Voices of Influence
Volume 4

Jen Loving

Published by
Hybrid Global Publishing
333 E 14th Street
#3C
New York, NY 10003

Manufactured in the United States of America, or in the United Kingdom when distributed elsewhere.

Loving, Jen
Engaging Speakers Voices of Influence

Paperback ISBN: 978-1-967598-00-7
E-book ISBN: 978-1-967598-01-4

Cover design by: Natasha Clawson
Copyediting by: Claudia Volkman
Interior design by: Suba Murugan

Contents

Introduction

Jen Loving

In a world filled with countless voices, the most powerful messages often emerge from those willing to share their unique perspectives and experiences. *Voices of Influence* is a testament to this bravery, showcasing the profound insights of fifteen remarkable authors, each committed to inspiring and impacting lives through their work.

As the CEO of Engaging Speakers, I have had the privilege of witnessing firsthand the transformative power of storytelling. This compilation unites a diverse array of voices, all driven by the desire to make a difference. Within these pages, you will find stories that challenge the status quo, wisdom that ignites passion, and practical insights that empower action.

Whether you are an entrepreneur seeking guidance, a leader striving for growth, or an individual yearning for inspiration, this book offers invaluable lessons and perspectives that can help you navigate your own path. Each author has poured their heart and soul into their contributions, providing a rich tapestry of experiences designed to uplift and motivate.

As you explore these pages, I encourage you to reflect on the messages that resonate with you. Allow yourself to be moved by their stories, and let their insights guide you toward your own path of influence. Together, let's celebrate the power of voices that inspire change and foster growth. Welcome to *Voices of Influence*!

Jen Loving is the CEO of Engaging Speakers, a successful business coach, and a bestselling author with ten books. She has generated more than $25 million in sales, raised more than $1 million in donations for nonprofits, and helped thousands of entrepreneurs to build their businesses, with many reaching six- and seven-figure revenues. She has been featured on Inc.com, *ABC News*, and in the *Chicago Tribune*, and has spoken on stage to more than ten thousand people. She is most proud of founding her own international nonprofit, Handing Hope, which brings comfort and smiles to children battling cancer. Jen resides outside of Chicago with her four incredible kids and Raider, the family dog.

From Seattle to Satoshi Island: The Price of Being Prescient

Dr. Alex Cahana

When I was asked in 2008 to run the Division of Pain Medicine at the University of Washington in Seattle, the first multidisciplinary pain clinic in the world, little did I know I would spend most of my time fighting my colleagues over the consequences of unintentional deaths from painkiller overdoses.

As a professor, this was supposed to be the zenith of my twenty-year academic career. When the medical director of the Department of Labor and Industries of the State of Washington called me, concerned that prescribed high-dose opioids (like oxycontin) were killing injured workers, I gladly started to work with him and other state agencies, private practicing physicians, and the University of Washington to author the first US professional prescription guidelines that eventually reversed these devastating trends.

Encouraged from these initial successes, I proceeded to support state legislation efforts (HB2876) to codify these guidelines. However, I underestimated the strong negative feedback I would receive from my colleagues, professional pain organizations, patient advocacy groups, and even a menacing nine-figure lawsuit from the pill manufacturer (which was later overturned).

Within weeks, I found myself thrown off every national committee and professional pain society. I even appeared in *The New York Times* as the "mean doctor that doesn't want to prescribe drugs." But nothing couldn't have been further from the truth. All I wanted was to make sure that prescriptions were done correctly, judiciously, and safely and introduce the idea that maybe there are other ways to treat pain besides pill popping.

For the next decade and despite ongoing skepticism and resistance, I continued to tenaciously disseminate our guidelines and data, as more and more stakeholders adopted our approach, including the Department of Defense (DoD), the Department of Veterans Affairs (VA), and the Center for Disease Control (CDC). In particular, I insisted that measuring patient-reported outcomes at every clinical encounter and avoiding high-dose prescriptions for non-cancer pain were essential for these guidelines to have an effect.

I advocated using complementary methods to treat pain such as naturopathic and plant medicine, acupuncture, traditional Chinese and Ayurvedic medicine, mindfulness, hypnosis, and meditation. I helped successfully open the Defense-Veterans Center for Integrative Pain Management (DVCIPM) to treat all service members and their families.

Though this chapter has a happy ending, the manufacturer settled for $7.5 billion, many of the plaintiffs retired and the societies that sued me dismantled after proven to be a front for irresponsible practice, and I learned my first lesson in being prescient: If you come up with something new, don't expect people to support you, especially when it hurts their bottom line.

My second lesson came when I moved to New York City in 2014 to focus on redesigning the US healthcare system. Though there are many problems with healthcare, I think I can sum up these issues in eight words: *We pay too much and die too young.*

Not only that, but everyone is unhappy. From a patient point of view, healthcare is too expensive; from a healthcare professional's perspective, there are too many administrative hassles; for hospital executives, the unchecked consolidation has not translated into better patient outcomes. The future of pharma and digital therapies is fraught with uncertainty, and even insurance companies are experiencing increased scrutiny of their "do not pay for care" policies.

How does one even start to "fix" this kind of system? Well, step one, just like with patients, diagnose where the pain is. Once done, it is necessary to understand the drivers of the system's "pain" and where lies the resistance to get better. Finally, what is considered a successful outcome?

Using this framework, it is not hard to diagnose the US healthcare disease. It suffers from affluenza, meaning overtreatment is the new undertreatment. The system is a $5T centralized economy that benefits from a "test for every pest and a pill for every ill." In fact, treating patients, especially those suffering from chronic disease, and getting them healthy is "bad for business." So much so that any discussion on "fixing" the system is muted. Personally, I think there is nothing to fix. The system is doing exactly what it is designed to do: to keep you sick, or at least sick enough.

That's when I learned my second lesson: Not every pain is bad, and not every pain relief is good. I realized we need a completely new healthcare system—the opposite system to the centralized one we have. We need decentralized healthcare.

But what does that mean? Well, when we speak about decentralized healthcare, what we are really talking about is the decentralization of healthcare data. Anyone who ever wanted to read, take, or transfer data from their electronic health record to another knows how hard, if not impossible, that is. Our health data, although extremely valuable, is shrouded with secrecy, many times unobtainable, and even worse, lost.

In addition, centralizing health data makes it vulnerable to hacking, censorship, and collusion, and data in silos prevent cooperation, collaborative innovation, and research. But in my opinion, the source of all the US healthcare system dysfunction is that healthcare data is in the hands of a few—and that only benefits the few and encourages continuing this misaligned economy.

Once I understood that, I left the world of pain medicine to dive deep into an unknown, new world of decentralized technologies: the world of blockchain, cryptocurrencies, and token economics. Initially, the bad reputation of crypto did not make things any easier. Now there are legitimate reasons to replace healthcare databases such as the Uniform Hospital Discharge Data Set (UHDDS); the Uniform Ambulatory Care Data Set (UACDS); the Minimum Data Set for long-term care (MDS); the Data Elements for Emergency Department Systems (DEEDS); the Outcomes and Assessment Information Set (OASIS); and the Health Plan Employer Data and Information Set (HEDIS). These multiple centralized databases have proven to be vulnerable, expensive, and unable to provide the integrated insights necessary for personalized, safe, and efficient care. Therefore, Distributed Ledger Technology (DLT)—and most notably blockchain—actually provides a secure, immutable, decentralized alternative to share and transact data.

Because healthcare systems use a shared repository (EHRs) with multiple writers (doctors, nurses, staff) and transaction dependencies (adherence to treatment plans, payments, regulations) with multiple intermediaries (professionals, patients, payors, regulators) that have no or minimal trust between them, blockchain is a perfect solution. It makes the need for trust obsolete and remedies many of these data and incentive shortcomings.

The problem is that many, if not most, healthcare professionals and associates have low levels of digital literacy and are misinformed about crypto. Thus, they are incapable of conceiving, let alone imagining, a systemic solution to the current problems.

And this is where I learned my third lesson: Things take time.

The reason it takes time is that change always follows the five steps of grief, eloquently described by Dr. Elisabeth Kübler-Ross, namely: Denial (no one at first believed me, or understood what is the utility of blockchain); Anger (we see so much misinformation on media about crypto); Bargaining (only now crypto is being discussed in Congress); Depression (many fear crypto will harm our future economy), and Acceptance (soon everyone will adopt crypto, and crypto wallets and dapps will simply be wallets and apps).

Just as it took us a decade to convince the world that unintentional deaths from opioids were due to overprescription and that the old ways need to change, I think it will take a decade to show that decentralized health data will inevitably replace the current unsustainable centralized healthcare system we are forced to use.

Which brings me to my next lesson: You cannot seriously talk about mental and physical health without taking care of planet health and financial health. So as I was designing these decentralized healthcare systems, I found myself traveling around the world to East and West Africa, Latin American and the Caribbeans, Asia and the Pacific Islands. What started as decentralized healthcare system design slowly morphed into building holistic, decentralized communities—such as Satoshi Island.

Traditionally known as Lataro Island, Satoshi Island is one of the more than eighty islands in the Melanesian country of Vanuatu. There we are building a regenerative, eco-conscious, smart community intended to accommodate intentional travelers, digital nomads, conservationists, technologists, entrepreneurs, and Web3 enthusiasts. Obviously, the untouched, pristine, tax-free environment was appealing, but what made Satoshi Island and a dozen more locations special is that they are all a combination of high-tech, high-touch, in-touch ecotopias.

These provide a coexisting alternative to the diminishing quality of life in urban communities and nation-states. Decentralized communities with an innovative mission, capacity for action, consensus governance, integrated cryptocurrency, and crowdfunded lands, offer co-living conditions for those looking to replace incivility, radicalization, and centralized surveillance.

Decentralized communities are controlled by no one and owned by the commons. They follow two core values: a regenerative design, supporting sustainable and restorative practices; and data transparency, engendering transactional trust. These capabilities mimic nature (bio-mimicking), and incorporate ancestral, indigenous knowledge as well as technological, decentralized infrastructure.

Life on Satoshi Island and like-minded places also challenge the idea of ownership. When I think of property, I think of possessive individualism. I think of "stuff" that belongs to me, discrete from "your stuff," governed by laws, bureaucracy, and enforcement. This form of ownership creates a rivalrous and extractive relationship between me, my neighbors, the community, and the planet at an onerous, unsustainable cost.

But there is another way to create ownership where resources are shared, economic disparity is minimized, and the focus is on communal well-being rather than individual gain. It's a way where members transparently contribute their goods and services to a commitment pool (an economic commons) and in return not only receive other goods and services (bartering), but also transform informal promises (commitments) into tangible assets (Real-World Assets), like citizen and land digital certificates called non-fungible tokens (NFTs).

Citizen NFTs represent adherence to commitments like sharing resources, pooled labor, positive economic engagement, regenerative and peaceful living, and cultural preservation of the island. Land NFTs represent a time-limited opportunity (lease) to develop the land through partial common ownership, incentivized and rewarded by means such as land value tax (more development, less tax), demurrage (charges for delays), and revenue sharing with other land NFT holders and community members.

As you can see, land NFTs do not represent the right to infinite ownership where you can exclude everyone from using your land as long as you wish, even if you do not use it in any productive way. Instead, it's rewarding virtuous development, property stewardship, prioritizing community benefits, and preventing labor exploitation and land degradation. Furthermore, commitment pooling coordinates land management efforts and creates an economy that accelerates land improvement.

And what about social order? Regenerative design in these communities allows us to promote individual and collective growth, while transparency, trust, and tokenization allow us to collaborate and attain a higher order of civility. New economic models like electronic bartering, reciprocal gifting, collective saving, cooperative, committed and parametric pooling mean not only attaching value to what we do (land NFTs, Satoshi Island coins), but more importantly represent who we are, incentivizing us to be the best version of ourselves (citizen NFTs).

Decentralized communities like Satoshi Island are not for everyone. They are places only for those who seek to "peer" fairly, to "pool" transparently, and to passionately co-create. They exist to cure our nihilistic narrative of individualism that has led us to endemic isolation, deep polarity, and deaths of despair. In these places we can collectively access nature, and through it, become human again.

This brings me to my final lesson: Let's stop loving things and using people and go back to how it should be. Let's love people and use things.

If this is the only lesson you will remember from my story, then all the angst, misunderstanding, jealousy, and hate of being ahead of my time makes the price of being prescient worth it.

Dr. Alex Cahana specializes in Web3 technology and builds decentralized communities in Africa, Latin America, and the Asian Pacific. With thirty years of clinical experience, Dr. Cahana consults with early-stage companies, investors, and governments. He believes we should love people and use things, not the other way around.

https://www.linkedin.com/in/dr-alex-cahana-health-blockchanger/

Looking to join a community of eco-conscious entrepreneurs, technologists, Web3 enthusiasts, and investors, where business brilliance meets deep self-awareness? Curious to build with intentional travelers, digital nomads, and conservationists a high-tech, high-touch, in-touch environment designed to co-create, co-laborate and co-experience spiritual growth? If yes, read my posts and reach out to me on LinkedIn.

From Breakdown to Breakthrough: Escaping the Corporate Grind for a Life of Purpose

Chris Conant

After leaving the corporate world, it took me five years to find my way. There were many dark times during this journey when giving up felt like the only option as I tried to make sense of my circumstances. I faced numerous challenges in my quest for a life that was indeed my own. During those years, I stumbled through various opportunities and fell into countless pitfalls. Those five years were filled with self-doubt and fear. Today, I am determined to help others avoid falling off the cliff as I once did.

For more than twenty-five years, I was trapped in the corporate grind, moving between the banking, sales, and client service industries. From scrappy startups to Fortune 500 giants, I climbed the ladder across England, Canada, and the US. Yet no matter how high I climbed or how hard I worked, I never felt truly valued or given the opportunities I knew I deserved. Like so many of us, I was conditioned to believe there was only one path to success: school, college, job, marriage, a house, kids, and decades of corporate servitude until retirement. We are told to feel lucky for our two weeks of vacation, to fit our families and passions around the demands of our jobs, and to accept that this is just how life is.

Not too long ago, I was living the corporate high life, a poster child for success in the fast-paced world of global finance. I had climbed the ladder in some of the largest markets worldwide, holding high-level positions adorned with all the trappings of power and shiny golden handcuffs. My days were spent on bustling trading floors and in some of the world's most prestigious companies. Nights turned into a whirlwind of wining and dining with clients, jetting off to international meetings in business class, and staying in luxury accommodations. I had it all—a private office, an expense account, and more invitations to exclusive events than I could count. I was a regular in private boxes at sporting events, rubbing shoulders with the elite and powerful. To the outside world, I was the epitome of success, a living testament to the power of hard work and determination.

But appearances can be deceiving.

What if I pulled back the curtain and revealed the reality behind this façade of success? What if I told you about the sleepless nights spent staring at the ceiling, my mind racing with deadlines and deliverables? Or the gripping anxiety of another long commute, questioning my sanity? What about the growing chasm between me and the people I loved most—a gap widening with each missed school event and half-hearted "I'm sorry, but this project is crucial"?

Like many others, I could push through. Admitting I needed help felt like a weakness, and in the ruthless corporate world, weakness was like blood in the water. So I pushed harder, worked longer, and ignored the warning signs as my world began to crumble around me, piece by piece. It started small—missing a child's milestone at home because of a last-minute meeting—but each missed moment became a brick in the wall growing between me and what mattered most, a wall I was too blind or scared to recognize.

Days turned into years, and my promises to myself and my family became as empty as the bottles of bourbon I'd begun to rely on to "unwind" after work. The liquor burned going down, but it was nothing compared to the burning shame I felt every time I looked in the mirror, seeing not the successful executive I pretended to be but the failure of a husband and father I had become.

My marriage was once a place of encouragement and happiness, but together, we descended into the trenches of anger and misunderstanding. My wife's pleas for me to "just talk to her" fell on deaf ears. I was too busy, too significant, and too afraid—afraid of admitting that I was drowning, fearful of showing vulnerability, terrified of confronting the mess I'd made of my personal life. Instead, I chose to escape the chaos through my unhealthy vices.

And those precious early years with my children that everyone tells you to savor passed by like sand through an hourglass. That fleeting time is gone forever. I was trading away our present for an increasingly empty and meaningless future.

My escape from the corporate world was anything but graceful. It came after a mental breakdown that nearly cost me everything. The relentless commutes, the feeling of insignificance, and the realization I was just another cog in a machine that would keep turning with or without me became overwhelming.

In December 2019, I left the office in a daze. My head spinning, I was empty of emotion or energy, functioning on autopilot. I endured the long, dreary commute home and walked through the front door. Almost immediately, I turned around, realizing I needed to get to the hospital before I did something terrible to myself—something irreversible. As I drove to the hospital, I was tempted to run red lights and plunge straight into the water. That thought felt so peaceful—how it would quiet the noise in my head.

But as I drove, something unexpected happened. Something stopped me from going through with it and held me at the traffic lights. So many thoughts raced through my mind, although the positive ones won this time. For the first time in as long as I could remember, my kids, wife, and family occupied my thoughts, and I made it to the hospital instead.

I didn't know whether to cry or yell when I waited alone in that small room. In the end, I did neither. My body felt empty and exhausted. I needed someone to guide me again, to show me the way back before it was too late.

The next few hours became a blur of questions, assessments, and decisions. I felt exposed, every carefully constructed façade torn away. Yet behind the fear and humiliation was light . . . hope. For the first time in years, I didn't have to pretend everything was fine. I could finally acknowledge that I was broken and in doing so, take the first step toward putting myself back together again.

When I got home, my wife was there, and it was tough bringing up my visit to the hospital. However, for the first time in a long while, though our conversation was awkward and off-balance, I felt more at ease with her than when we were getting along perfectly.

As I sat there, speechless after sharing my story, her eyes filled with pity and relief. At that moment, I realized how wrong I had been to want to face this alone. The road ahead was still filled with difficulties, but when she held out her hand to take mine, I understood we still had a fragile yet healthy connection.

What followed was eighteen months of long-term disability, countless therapy sessions, and a desperate search for meaning. I explored hobbies that turned into businesses, immersed myself in job interviews I'm now grateful I didn't get, and constantly battled the pull of the corporate matrix that had led me to rock bottom in the first place.

The first time I visited a therapist's office was tough. I was so used to being in control of my life that it felt strange and awkward to give up control to someone else, even though I had none. How could I, a man who prided himself on always being in control, admit I was lost? But as the weeks passed, something unusual happened. I began peeling away some layers of who I thought I should be, revealing a different person. It wasn't easy. There were times I yelled into the void about how unfair everything seemed, and other times I cried like a baby.

Psychotherapy isn't just for the "crazier" among us; it's a tool for anyone who wants to live life to the fullest and achieve balance. It has been key in helping me discover who I truly am and who I wish to become.

Step by step, I started to understand myself in new ways. I confronted the fears and insecurities from my childhood that drove me to seek validation through my work. Slowly but surely, I began rebuilding. My wife and I started dating again—actually dating, not just grabbing quick meals between my meetings. We laughed and cried together, rediscovering the early days of our love. However, progress was slow; it took several years to heal those wounds and breathe normally again. Yet every honest conversation and every time we leaned on each other paved the way forward.

As for my kids, they now see me for who I truly am. I attend all their games, whether as a coach or a spectator; I help with their homework; and I have time to talk with them about anything, anytime. I am rediscovering the joy of being a father, one ordinary moment at a time. We sold our house, lived with relatives, and had to start over from scratch. Yet with every move we made, we rebuilt our lives.

I was never sure whether leaving the corporate jungle was a good idea. I lay awake at night, wondering if all my working days had been wasted. It wasn't easy to give up a steady paycheck and the work I had put in throughout my twenty-five years. Was it all for nothing? Yet, as I began to focus on what mattered—the state of my health, my family, and my creative work—something remarkable started to happen. I began to see opportunities I had not appreciated before.

Even though I made several attempts at entrepreneurship and seemed to throw good money after bad, the experience was worth every penny. I can see now that it was an investment in my education, which taught me what is needed to run a successful business. This was the knowledge I needed all along. Running a company that would resonate with one of my key core values: helping people. The greater the success of every busy corporate executive or professional athlete I work with, the more convinced I become that I am on the right track.

It wasn't all smooth sailing, of course. I had to develop skills for managing my own time and dealing with the uncertainty of entrepreneurship. I had to find new ways—different from anything that had worked before—to balance work and family. But I enjoy my new career more than ever. When I wake up in the morning, I feel no regret. Golden handcuffs don't mean much compared to the chance to do something you love.

Financially, it's been a roller coaster. At times I didn't know how my family and I would make ends meet for months. However strong the temptation to return to the safety of corporate life became, I had my whole family behind me. We learned to live with necessities and discovered the joys of experiences over possessions. Little by little, as my business began to prosper, we got back on track and started doing well. Thankfully, I had my wonderful wife, who helped support the family finances while I made this change.

Today, I stand before you, not as a perfect man but as a man in progress. I have exchanged my private office for a life filled with purpose and connection. Instead of long nights at the office or out on the town, I end my days with good stories, laughs, and family dinners. I have never been as happy or fulfilled in all my life!

The success my company and I have seen in helping others with our 90-Day Escape program is proof that many others have struggles like I once did. The 90-Day Escape helps executives who feel stuck find their way. Maybe it's moving up, perhaps it's moving out, but there's a way to live a life you love in a career that fills you with joy. I am determined to help as many people as possible.

Transitioning from being a stressed-out corporate worker to a life rich with meaning may not have been easy, but every step was worth it, and for once, the road ahead is bright.

Chris Conant specializes in coaching individuals ready to break free from their current roles and step into careers filled with purpose, passion, and profit. With years of experience guiding athletes, entrepreneurs, and corporate professionals, Chris brings a unique approach combining strategic planning, mindset transformation, and actionable steps.

cconant.com

Ready to make your own escape? Head over to cconant.com/voices for an exclusive free resource that will guide you toward more purpose, freedom, and fulfillment in both your career and personal life. Your next chapter starts now!

Between Extremes

Brad Feinberg

In today's world, the conversation around body acceptance is both liberating and often deeply problematic. On one end of the spectrum, influencers preach radical acceptance of obesity as though it were a badge of honor while ignoring the undeniable health risks that come with it. On the opposite end, we're bombarded with images of skeletal thinness—an equally dangerous ideal that's often cloaked in hashtags like #fitspo or #goals. Somewhere in the middle of these extremes lies a truth that's difficult to market but vital to embrace: balance.

Over the last two decades as a health and fitness coach, I've seen these extremes manifest in ways that are both heartbreaking and at times infuriating. I've worked with celebrities whose livelihoods depend on their appearance, high-powered business leaders who are as driven in the boardroom as they are in the gym, and everyday high performers who just want to feel good in their own skin. In all of them, I've witnessed the same struggle: the fight between their inner voice and the external narrative society pushes on them.

The truth is, body acceptance isn't about resigning yourself to being unhealthy or chasing an unattainable aesthetic. It's about finding a balance that honors your physical and mental health—a place where self-respect meets self-awareness. But in a culture that thrives on extremes, balance often feels like a revolutionary act, or worse, like you're playing for the losing team in a game no one remembers signing up for. Striving for balance is choosing to sidestep the landmines of societal expectations and instead create your own definition of health—one that doesn't require starving yourself into oblivion or treating lettuce like it's a cheat meal. Balance isn't glamorous, but it's the only way to keep yourself from becoming a casualty of cultural extremes.

The Dangerous Lies of "It's OK to Be Fat"

Let's start with the elephant in the room—literally and figuratively. The so-called "body positivity" movement, which began as a way to celebrate diversity in body shapes and sizes—a noble and necessary goal—has in some corners morphed into something else entirely. It's one thing to say, "You are worthy of love and respect regardless of your size." It's another to glorify being overweight or obese as if it were without consequence. Because, let's be honest, there's a fine line between embracing your curves and pretending your cardiologist doesn't exist.

I've trained clients whose health markers were in the red zone—blood pressure through the roof, cholesterol levels screaming for attention, joints buckling under excess weight. Every step felt like a negotiation with their knees, and sleep came only in fits and starts, interrupted by the suffocating grip of sleep apnea. Yet they'd been lulled into complacency by influencers telling them it's fine to stay as they are. "Self-love" had been twisted into self-neglect. One client confessed they hadn't seen a doctor in years because they didn't want to hear bad news, as if ignorance could somehow silence their body's warning cries. Another spoke about how they used to joke about being "fluffy" until their toddler asked why they were always too tired to play.

Acceptance doesn't mean ignoring the warning signs your body is sending you. Real love is taking care of yourself, not letting yourself deteriorate because someone on Instagram told you it's "courageous" to do so. Courage isn't about denying reality; it's about facing it head-on and choosing to do better—even when it's hard. Because when your body gives up, no amount of online validation can hold it together. And trust me, there's nothing brave about finding yourself in an ER at 3:00 a.m., clutching your chest and hoping the paramedics are fast enough.

But hey, if you're content to keep your arteries playing Russian roulette, that's your call. Just know that when your chest starts feeling like it's hosting a drum solo at 2:00 a.m., those inspirational Instagram captions aren't going to dial 911 for you.

The Obsession with Perfection

On the flip side, we have the fitness industry, where perfection isn't just an ideal—it's a currency. The six-pack has become the symbol of fitness, regardless of what lies beneath it. I've seen people destroy their bodies in pursuit of this ideal. From crash diets that leave them perpetually fatigued to anabolic steroids and diuretics that ravage their organs, the price of chasing "perfection" is steep. And for what? A photo, a fleeting sense of validation, a few more likes?

Even in my own career, I've felt the pull of this toxic mindset. Touring with celebrities, there was an unspoken pressure to "look the part," as if my expertise and ability to transform others didn't matter unless I also looked like I'd just stepped off the cover of *Men's Health*. That pressure led me down a dangerous path. I started experimenting with performance-enhancing drugs, chasing an image of perfection I thought would validate my worth as a coach and a professional.

When you play God with your endocrine system, the negative side effects can be absolutely brutal. I'm not just talking about the physical toll—although the acne, mood swings, and constant fatigue were enough to make me question my sanity. It was the mental and emotional unraveling that hit the hardest. I became obsessed with the mirror, measuring every inch of progress with a mix of pride and paranoia. My self-esteem became tethered to whether I could maintain the "look," and the more I chased it, the further away I felt from the person I wanted to be.

The irony was inescapable: I was destroying my health to sell the image of health. It wasn't until I hit rock bottom—mentally and physically—

that I realized how far I'd strayed from my values. Recovering from that period wasn't easy, but it taught me an invaluable lesson: There is no shortcut to balance. The moment you sacrifice your health for an image, you've already lost the game. Now, I share this story not as a cautionary tale to scare you, but as a reminder that perfection is a lie, and chasing it will take more from you than it will ever give.

The paradox is hard to ignore. The people who look the healthiest are often the ones struggling the most—not just physically, but mentally and emotionally. I've worked with individuals who, on the surface, seemed to have it all together: chiseled abs, bulging biceps, and flawless gym selfies. But beneath that polished exterior lay the truth: bodies pushed to the brink and minds burdened by the relentless pressure to maintain an image.

When I first met one client, who was pursuing the Men's Physique lifestyle, he shared that he couldn't remember the last time he felt truly happy. His hormones were in shambles, his energy levels were nonexistent, and he was constantly battling anxiety about whether he looked "good enough."

Another high performer I coached confessed to feeling trapped by his own success. He had the physique people envied but couldn't escape the nagging fear that he'd lose it if he relaxed even for a moment. Every meal was calculated, every workout brutal, and every day felt like a test he was destined to fail.

The irony cuts deep because, on the surface, these men appeared to be the pinnacle of health. But underneath the facade, it's a different story: a constant sense of inadequacy, hormonal chaos, and an overwhelming sense of isolation. It's a reminder that chasing perfect aesthetics at all costs isn't just unsustainable—it's self-sabotage disguised as discipline. And while their feeds might scream "inspiration," their bodies and minds are quietly crying out for help.

Now, don't get me wrong: There is a time and place for proper hormone and peptide therapy. When done under the guidance of qualified professionals, these treatments can be life-changing for those with legitimate medical needs. Hormone therapy can restore vitality, improve quality of life, and address issues that diet and exercise alone can't fix. But—and this is a critical but—it's all about balance. The line between therapy and abuse is razor-thin, and crossing it to chase perfection is where things go dangerously wrong. Properly guided treatments can help you optimize your health; abusing them can leave you battling side effects that make the original problem seem trivial. The goal should never be perfection but rather a balanced and sustainable approach to well-being.

The Power of Listening to Yourself

One of my clients embodied a philosophy that has stayed with me for years: Success, in any realm, comes from tuning out external noise and focusing on what truly matters—your inner voice. That mindset extended to his health and fitness. He wasn't chasing a six-pack or trying to conform to someone else's definition of "healthy." Instead, he focused on what made him feel strong, sharp, and energized— qualities that fueled his ability to lead and innovate at the highest level. By turning inward and aligning his health goals with his personal priorities, he achieved a level of balance that wasn't flashy but was undeniably effective. It was never about aesthetics for him; it was about functionality, longevity, and a sense of well-being that couldn't be quantified by a mirror or a scale. But because he listened inwardly, he also looked like a god.

Contrast that with a business leader who came to me after years of yo-yo dieting and overtraining. He had been trapped in a cycle of trying to meet the impossible standards of public perception, constantly worried that any deviation from his strict regimen would be seen as a personal failure. His identity was so deeply intertwined with his appearance that even the smallest weight fluctuation felt like a crisis. Over time, this obsession had drained him—mentally, physically, and emotionally. It wasn't until he shifted his focus to prioritize his well-being over external approval that he discovered what true balance looked like. By listening to his body and redefining health on his own terms, he not only improved his physical fitness but also reclaimed his peace of mind. And ironically, he's never looked or felt better.

Falling in Love with Who You Become

The key to lasting health and happiness isn't in following the latest trend or bowing to societal pressure. It's in discovering what balance looks like for you. When you stop chasing extremes and start listening to your body, you'll be amazed at what it's capable of. Achieving this balance doesn't mean avoiding challenges; it means incorporating the right intensity and progressive overload into your routine to grow stronger and more resilient. Pushing yourself appropriately, while allowing time for recovery and adjustment, is the sweet spot where true progress happens. This balance of effort and rest ensures not only physical growth but also mental clarity and long-term sustainability.

This isn't about settling. It's about striving—not for perfection but for progress. It's about respecting your body enough to challenge it and care for it in equal measure. And it's about falling in love with who you become when you stop living for others and start living for yourself.

Balance doesn't sell. Extremes do. Nobody's making TikToks about their balanced and healthy lifestyle—there's no clickbait in consistency, no viral appeal in a life that's quietly thriving. But the space where health and fulfillment intersect is where the magic happens. It's where you stop living to impress and start living to thrive. It's where health becomes less about aesthetics and more about longevity—less about perfection and more about progress. This powerful intersection is where you find the freedom to enjoy life without constantly punishing yourself in the pursuit of unattainable standards.

And while it may not get you a million followers or a viral hashtag, it will get you something far more valuable: peace. Peace with your body, peace with your choices, and peace with knowing you're living a life that's sustainable and fulfilling. Because at the end of the day, it's not the highlight reels on social media that define your happiness—it's the quiet moments when you feel strong, healthy, and unapologetically yourself.

In a world of extremes, balance is the ultimate rebellion. So rebel. Honor your health, listen to your inner voice, and let go of the noise. Because the only opinion that truly matters is your own.

Brad Feinberg, a health and wellness expert with an exercise physiology degree, has coached CEOs, entertainers, and global brands. Overcoming type 1 diabetes and addiction, he emphasizes the mind-body connection for transformative results. He has become the mastermind behind several celebrities' body makeovers, including Dan Reynolds, Benson Boone, Susie Abromeit, and Steve Aoki.

bradfeinberg.com

Ready for the next step? Head over to bradfeinberg.com/voices to unlock a powerful free resource designed to spark real change. Discover actionable strategies and get exclusive insights to help you break free from extremes and build lasting, balanced health—starting right now.

Surpassing Expectations: Empowering Children with Down Syndrome in Their First Twenty-Four Months

Linda Franklin-Biggs

Every baby's early transformative years are full of incredible potential, and the first twenty-four months of life offer an amazing window of opportunity to lay the foundation for significant future success. This is equally true for babies with Down syndrome. Some of the biggest challenges children with Down syndrome face in learning need to be addressed as early as possible to garner long-term results. Even with the hurdles of low muscle tone, proportionately smaller ear canals, and frequent fluid buildup in the ear, the good news is that parents and caregivers can help their baby right from birth.

I'll be sharing the "what, why, and how" in this chapter. Included will be the critical role of early communication and how parents and caregivers can foster and encourage early communication beginning at birth. I'll share the concept of synapse pruning that takes place in the human brain at twenty-four months, and I'll explain why the term *use it or lose it* applies.

A little about my journey in this area. It all started with an experiment I did with my own granddaughter from 2013 to 2016. This experiment stemmed from a vocal pedagogy class I took for my master's degree. I didn't know anything about the instructor, Dr. Brenda Smith, PhD.

I soon learned that she had won national awards in both science and music areas, along with Dr. Robert Sataloff, MD, DMA, FACS, for their research on the voice. The purpose of this class was to train music teachers how to teach children to sing on pitch and how to keep the voice healthy. I learned so much more!

For their research, Dr. Robert Sataloff had placed a tiny camera up the nose and down the throat of Dr. Brenda Smith to observe and record her vocal cords. I got to watch this video and see exactly how the vocal cords work. The most amazing thing I learned from their research was that when Dr. Sataloff sang, it actually moved Dr. Smith's vocal muscles to try and match the shape of his!

Taking this information back to the public school classroom, I no longer used the piano when teaching children the notes to a new song. When children would sing off pitch, I simply sang and modeled the correct pitches for them again, knowing that my voice was moving their muscles to match the shape of mine. Sometimes I had to model it multiple times, but it worked. I was amazed at the results I got! That year my students performed at a whole new level. My colleagues made comments like "You got lucky this year," assuming the children came to me with these beautiful singing voices and all I did was teach them the songs. They didn't know better. After several years of this, finally the gym teacher said to me, "Linda, I don't know how you do it, but every year the kids sound great!" After practicing these vocal techniques with children in the classroom and seeing how effective they were, I thought, *This must be how babies learn how to talk!* I couldn't wait until I had a grandchild to test out my hypothesis.

In the meantime, I moved to a school that served pre-kindergarten through second grade students. An experience I had with a preschooler with Down syndrome led me to write my master's degree thesis on the effects of music on preschool children with Down syndrome. Maggie (not her real name) had Down syndrome and was wheeled into my class in a wooden high chair. When the para educator took her out of the chair to join the class, she immediately ran off. The para educator would chase her, bring her back, and she would run off again; this went on for weeks. It didn't appear that Maggie was actually learning anything. After some time, Maggie's mother called her special education teacher to inquire about the hand motions and songs Maggie was trying to do at home. They were the songs and activities I had been teaching her class! She *had* been learning despite her running off and seemingly not paying attention. Children do not have to be facing you and giving you what appears to be their undivided attention in order to learn.

In July 2013, my granddaughter, Brooklynn, was born. I decided to try an experiment. I thought that if my voice moves her muscles, then I could ultimately strengthen her muscles enough for her to start talking early. How do you strengthen any muscle? Expand and contract the muscle repeatedly, that's how! By singing high, the vocal cords stretch out long and thin, and by singing low they get very small, round, and fat. I decided to follow this train of thought. I began singing to Brooklynn every day. I'd sing the alphabet multiple times per day. I'd sing made-up songs, greetings, and storybooks; I also began reading lessons at two weeks old. Within five minutes of her first lessons, she fell asleep, yet I continued reading, knowing that her muscles were still able to absorb and respond. After ten months of singing daily, doing all sorts of classical and traditional lullaby music, reading, and lots of interactive and multisensory activities, Brooklynn said, "ABC." I ran and got my camera to video-record this because I knew no one would believe it! Soon after, she said, "DEF." The peculiar thing is that she continued to say either ABC or DEF, but she didn't put the six letters together, and she didn't say another letter until she came out with the entire alphabet at the age of eighteen months. She was fully conversant at the age of twelve months. I have a video from her first birthday with her sitting in the highchair, picking up an eight-pack of playdough she received as a gift, and exclaiming, "It's so bwig!" She realized that the weight of the box caused her to say "bwig" instead of "big," so she dropped the box on her tray and reiterated, "It's so big!"

When Brooklynn went to the doctor for a sick visit around nineteen months old, as the pediatrician walked into the room, she said, "I'm sick! I need a doctor!"

The pediatrician responded, "I'm a doctor; I think I can help. What seems to be the matter?"

She shared all her symptoms, and the doctor said, "She's more articulate than the teenagers who come in here!"

Then Brooklynn asked the doctor if she would check her heart with the stethoscope. Shocked, the doctor confirmed, "Did she just say stethoscope?"

By twenty-four months, Brooklynn already knew the alphabet and could visually recognize all the letters. She knew the sounds of letters and began reading simple words. She could hold a pen or crayon and color well and was already doing pre-K schoolwork. The doctor labeled her "talented and gifted." I actually taught her all that stuff! How much was nature or nurture?

Later, I was in Cincinnati at a Leadership Summit and had lunch with a young couple. The mother is a neurologist, and the father is a computer scientist. They were expecting their first child. I told them all about my work with Brooklynn, the mindset needed, how it works, and what to do when their baby arrived. They sent me a video of their baby at twenty-seven months singing the entire alphabet and having a conversation with her dad. That was it—I needed to start sharing this information with others because anyone could do this! The question I was often asked was, "Why do you need to start right from birth?"

At birth the human brain has more brain cells than it will ever use in its lifetime. At the age of twenty-four months, the brain begins a natural process of synapse pruning, in which it starts eliminating synapses that are weak or not being used. Up to this point, a baby's brain is like an open canvas, quickly creating an abundance of neural connections in response to every experience, sound, interaction, and movement. This pruning increases the brain's efficiency, yet certain foundational skills, especially in areas of communication and sensory processing, become more limited. If neural connections related to communication haven't been consistently activated before this pruning phase, the brain may discard them, making it harder for a child to develop those skills later.

Another question I get is "Does this work with neuro-diverse children?" I heard about a baby named Ava, who has Down syndrome. Ava was also medically fragile and spent the first four months of her life in the hospital. I met with Ava's parents on Zoom and shared the mindset and foundation for what to do and how this works. I sent them materials, music links, lessons, and activities to do with Ava, and I followed up with age-appropriate materials as Ava grew. The diagnosis of Down syndrome alone can put a child at risk of being behind their peers by kindergarten. Staying in the hospital for the first four months of life sets a child further back because they don't get to experience the sights, sounds, and smells of home and have all the typical learning experiences. Ava's mom started working with her daughter. When I reached out on Ava's second birthday to check on how things were going, her mom said, "Ava's doing amazing! She loves music, and whenever I use the blender in the kitchen, she starts dancing, thinking it's music. But the most amazing thing about the fact that she can communicate is that we never get to the temper tantrum stage!" Temper tantrums are a common result of frustration when communication is a barrier. So now, instead of being behind her peers by age five, Ava is ahead of her peers at age two!

For babies with Down syndrome, who may already experience delays in neural development, this window of opportunity is especially critical. Starting early interventions at birth allows parents and caregivers to build and reinforce the pathways necessary for communication and learning. After pruning begins, learning new skills is still possible, but it often requires significantly more effort and time because the brain's capacity to create entirely new connections diminishes.

Tips for Encouraging Early Communication

First, begin singing and talking to your baby from birth continually. For babies with Down syndrome, a high-pitched voice can cut through fluid in the ear easier than a lower-pitched voice. Remember, your voice will strengthen their vocal muscles, so the more you sing, the stronger their vocal muscles will become. Get close to their ear so they can hear you better. Expose your child to lots of quality music, both lullabies and classical.

A baby's receptive language is far more developed than their expressive language, and they can understand things much earlier than you think. If you record your baby when they're babbling, sometimes you can clearly hear upon playback what isn't understandable to the regular ear. Repeating what your child says to you shows that you understand and confirms to the child they're on the right track. If they're babbling, talk back to them. Think about the context of what's happening and what they could possibly be saying. For example, at feeding time, talk about the food to the baby, and when they respond, watch their facial and body language to help you determine what they may be babbling, and then ask questions and confirm. For example: "Do you like bananas? Would you like some more? These are sweet, aren't they? What color are bananas? Bananas are yellow."

Start engaging your baby in conversation with questions and then answer the questions for them so they learn how to answer for themselves. Repetition is a huge key to learning at this age. You need to repeat yourself quite a lot, so embrace repetition. No matter what you are doing with your baby, make sure to use lots of descriptive words to build their vocabulary. Include as many of the senses simultaneously as possible. Multisensory learning builds strong synapses and ultimately strong communication skills.

Most importantly, make sure to speak intelligently to and around your baby. Whether it's intentional or unintentional, you are teaching your baby all the time.

Embrace this time, for it is where the smallest actions yield the greatest impacts.

Linda Franklin-Biggs is an early childhood development expert, internationally acclaimed speaker, and contributing author to the bestselling *Parenting Owners Manual.* Recently featured on Roku TV's *Proactive Parent Show* with leading neurologist Dr. Lankerani, Linda has spoken on prominent platforms worldwide, including *The Vera Thomas Show, The Mama Genius Summit* with Michelle DeKeyser, the *Family Matters Mega Summit,* the *Warrior Podcast (UK),* and the *Health, Wealth & Wisdom Summit.*

With more than thirty years of experience and more than five thousand students taught, Linda is dedicated to helping parents maximize the potential of their newborns during the crucial first twenty-four months. Through her innovative approach, Linda focuses on empowering parents to proactively foster strong neural connections and early communication skills, emphasizing the importance of engaging during this critical window of opportunity. Her work continues to inspire families worldwide, offering practical tools to proactively address the risk of developmental delays from birth.

babywisdom.org

Gift from Linda Franklin-Biggs Sing & Play: Songs and Activities for Optimal Baby Brain Development Link: **https://bit.ly/sing-and-play-bw**

The Power of Thought: How I Rebuilt My Life

Brandon Hebron

A man is but the product of his thoughts. What he thinks, he becomes.

—MAHATMA GANDHI

For years, my thoughts were my prison. Trapped in a cycle of negativity, I became the very thing I feared most: powerless, anxious, and lost. Around 970 million people worldwide struggle with mental health issues, with this number continuing to rise each year. To put this into perspective, this means that for every eight people who pass by you on your way to get your morning coffee, at least one of those people will be having one of the worst days of their life. I was one of those people. Mulling around in a perpetual state of hopelessness and constantly worrying about what's next—or in my darkest moments, not caring at all. My personal antagonists were anxiety and depression. Every day was a constant struggle between feeling discouraged with virtually no plausible cause, paired with an overwhelming feeling of worry and stress.

Growing up, I wasn't the star student or the one everyone looked up to in school. My grades were mediocre at best, and I often felt like I was simply going through the motions, not excelling in any area. It wasn't that I didn't try; I simply wasn't as naturally gifted as some of my peers. Still, I graduated high school and went to Marquette—a medium-sized university in Milwaukee. I was a young, excitable freshman, eager to begin my new chapter and have the freedom to do what I wanted. However, my eagerness quickly faded as I began to experience the beginning stages of depression. Suddenly I found it nearly impossible to do anything. A seemingly easy task became difficult. I'd put off my homework until a not-so-friendly reminder would tell me the assignment was due at 11:59 p.m. that night, and my social life crumbled.

When you spend every day thinking nothing but negative thoughts, you eventually find yourself in a series of bad habits and even worse outcomes. Though I luckily never used hard drugs or ended up in jail, I found myself lost and confused with no aspirations or anything to look forward to. I reached a point where even a simple task such as going to the grocery store was difficult because I would worry about running into someone and being forced to have a conversation or, God forbid, make a mistake and say the wrong thing when checking out and embarrass myself. It was as if I were stranded at sea with no navigational equipment to lead me back home, my life decidedly in the hands of Mother Nature to determine which way the waves would take me. I didn't want to live this way anymore, but in some sick and twisted way, this was comfortable for me. It's what I knew. Life beyond that moment was scary because it was uncertain, and uncertainty can be a terrifying concept to wrap your head around.

Then, one day, my mindset was transformed. I was no longer stuck in that everlasting cycle of negative thinking and constant feeling of overcomplication. I began to adapt to a new way of thinking—one that is full of life and aspiration, constantly looking for ways to evolve and improve. Now, it wasn't literally one day. Looking back and reflecting on it, I can't really pinpoint the exact moment when my life began to change for the better. There was no epiphany where I said, "This is the day my life is going to change!" simply because this isn't the movies and that's not how life always works. Getting out of that perpetual state of hopelessness is not an overnight accomplishment but rather a slow and deliberate process of intentionally making very small but manageable steps forward. At the time, there was no real "end goal" per se. I wasn't the kid who wrote that they aspired to be an astronaut or a doctor in their elementary school yearbook. In fact, I have a piece of paper from second grade where I wrote I wanted to be an NBA or NFL player, even though I have never been the most athletic kid on the field. I didn't know where I wanted to be when I began my journey of self-development; I just knew I wanted out of that cycle, and knew I needed to make a change.

I come from a good background. My father is an exceptionally hardworking man who has raised me and my siblings to be very bright and talented individuals, all of whom have been equipped with the tools and knowledge necessary to become great at anything we do. Since birth he has constantly taught, and more importantly shown me, what it means to be successful in life, and even more so how to be a good father. He has led by example every step of the way and is living proof of someone I aspire to be.

Similarly, my mother is one of the strongest, most caring souls I have ever known. She has faced many obstacles in her life, but somehow she has always managed to come out stronger, and I've never seen her broken. There were many days when she would come home from a long day of work, stressed and unsatisfied beyond belief, only to immediately have to cook dinner for an entire family (we very likely may have revolted if she didn't—there simply is no substitution for her divine gift and ability to make incredibly delicious food). Yet she would still manage to hug me and my siblings and make us feel loved, as if the long and emotionally draining day never even happened. One hug from my mother, and I am instantly teleported back to my childhood, feeling overwhelmingly loved and appreciated without a care in the world. She, without knowing, has taught me the art of love and acceptance, and shown me what it means to truly care. Without her, I would not have the same level of gracefulness and empathy for others, which I have found are some of my best qualities. I have always been surrounded by people who love and care for me, and I am eternally grateful for the things they have done and the sacrifices they have made.

Over the years, I have come to realize that your life truly is in your hands. Though some situations outside of your control do take place, you ultimately get to decide what you want your life to look like and how you want to live it. I very easily could have continued to sulk and believe that nothing would ever change, leaving me stuck feeling hopeless and helpless. However, I made the decision to change and do what was necessary to pull myself out of that negative mindset. Deep thought comes naturally to me—a gift of anxiety, I guess. I would often find myself pondering about what I wanted my life to look like, and who I wanted to be. It's easy to forget, when you're in that paralyzing state of mind, that humans are, by nature, communal creatures, and we thrive by helping to lift others up. It's even easier to succumb to convince yourself you are completely alone and no one wants the burden of helping you.

However, I am here to tell you that that is simply not true. There is light on the other side of the tunnel, no matter how dark and void the space may seem right now. For me, this very slow and gradual process consisted of filling my brain with content from various motivational podcasts and self-help books. Some of my favorite podcasts to listen to included shows like *The Secret to Success*, *The Model Health Show*, and *Earn Your Leisure* (with a newfound favorite, *The Diary of a CEO*), all of which I still listen to consistently. These shows are led by some of the most inspirational and influential people in the world, and hearing their stories helped fuel the beginning of mine.

The journey to self-improvement is by no means a linear path. Throughout the years, I've encountered many bumps in the road and at times felt like I was moving backward. It's important to remember when crafting your own life's story that you will experience setbacks along the way and will need to remind yourself that it's OK. When overcoming an obstacle or a setback, you have to learn to recalibrate your thinking—whether that means setting smaller, more achievable goals, practicing mindfulness to regain perspective, or refocusing your mind on your end goal. For me, my end goal in life is to experience time and financial freedom so I can spend my days doing what I *want* to do rather than what I *have* to do. I want to put myself in a position to actively choose what is important to me instead of being forced to accept what is important to someone else. I want the ability to buy what I want, experience what I want, and live life the way I want. More importantly, I want to be able to spend my time in a way that is meaningful to me. Time is our greatest asset, and I desire to spend it on the things and people who mean the most to me.

Finding what drives you and identifying your purpose in life is, oddly enough, one of the most challenging things you can do, especially if you feel lost. Aligning yourself with who you want to be requires a certain level of openness and an exceptional ability to self-reflect. You must dig deep to uncover what it means to be you and visualize a path forward. Above all, you *must* learn the art of patience and understand that change takes time. Along the way, you'll face moments of doubt, times when you feel like you've lost your way again. It's easy to feel like you're not making progress, and sometimes, you'll want to give up. That's OK. Growth doesn't always feel like progress—it feels like discomfort, confusion, and uncertainty. But it's precisely in those moments of uncertainty that the most significant growth happens. In order to truly see the progress you're making, you have to know you are capable of making it happen. The key is persistence. Continue to move forward, even when you can't see the full picture. You have to trust that you have the strength and the skills to build the life you want—because you *do*. Your future is yours to create, and while the journey may be long and filled with setbacks, every small step you take brings you closer to living in your purpose.

Motivation is something you have to nurture, especially when you feel weak or stuck. It's not easy to keep going when it seems like you're not making progress, but that's when the smallest steps matter the most. Don't wait for motivation to strike out of nowhere—create it. Whether it's through small wins, positive affirmations, or just reminding yourself of why you started, it's those moments of self-encouragement that will fuel your progress. Rely on those around you, and seek guidance from those who are doing, or have done, what you are ultimately trying to accomplish. As you progress, remind yourself of where you've come from and offer to guide others along the way, as this will only help to propel yourself forward. That is why I recently created an Instagram page called Shift Your Momentum, which is dedicated to sharing motivational insights and wisdom that may help others on their journey. I have found that sharing motivation with others helps me to continue moving forward.

One of my all-time favorite quotes is the quote from Mahatma Gandhi at the beginning of this chapter. Think about that for a moment: The way you think shapes who you are and who you'll become. Every single one of us is the sum of our thoughts. So I ask you, do your thoughts reflect the person you truly want to be? If not, it's time for a change. Right now, in this very moment, you have the power to reshape your life. There is no better time than right now to start your transformation. The question is: Will you be the one to take the first step?

Brandon Hebron is a digital marketer, aspiring entrepreneur, and passionate advocate for positive change. Through mission work and youth programs, he uses his ability to connect with others to inspire growth, empower dreams, and help people live abundantly.

Shift Your Mindset, Change Your Life.
Want to break free from negative thought patterns? Get my free **Mindset Transformation Guide** with simple steps to build a growth mindset.

Email shiftyourmomentum@gmail.com with the subject line **"Mindset Shift"** to receive your copy!

Grandmothers Weaving the Fabric of Faith and Influence

Mimsy Hebron

Dedicated to my grandmothers Mary and Luvenia
Grandmothers live forever...

Episode 1

The morning sun spilled through the antique lace curtains of the little white house on Billow Street, painting the walls in warm hues of gold. In the kitchen, a symphony of scents wafted through the air . . . freshly baked buttermilk biscuits, crisp bacon, and the unmistakable aroma of coffee brewing in the pot. It was Sunday, and for the Johnson family that meant one thing: a day of faith, family, and fellowship.

At the heart of it all stood Grandma Maybell, her stout frame draped in a cobalt-blue dress underneath her white apron, her silver hair tied back neatly in a bun. Her hands moved with ease as she prepared breakfast for her family, humming an old hymn under her breath. "Great Is Thy Faithfulness" seemed to echo through the house, bathing each room with an intangible peace.

"Ya'll better get up! Church starts in an hour, and I'm not waiting for no stragglers," she called out, her voice firm but laced with love. One by one, her grandchildren stumbled into the kitchen, still rubbing sleep from their eyes. Ten-year-old Isaiah, with his unruly curls and mischievous grin, was the first to sneak a piece of bacon from the plate.

45

"Isaiah!" Grandma Maybell bellowed, pointing her wooden spoon at him, "You know better than to touch that before we pray."

He flashed her an apologetic toothy smile, the same one his mother used to get away with as a girl and shuffled to the table. Behind him came sixteen-year-old Ivy, earbuds in and scrolling through her phone, and finally their mother, Jasmine, who looked every bit as tired as a single mother of two might look.

"Morning, Mama," Jasmine said, kissing her mother softly on the cheek. "You need any help?" Maybell replied, her tone softening, "You can set the table and remind your daughter that we don't bring distractions to the Lord's house." Ivy rolled her eyes but obeyed, slipping the phone into her pocket as she said, "Yes, ma'am."

Grandma Maybell had a way of commanding respect without demanding it outright. It was in her unwavering faith, her steady presence, and the wisdom she carried like a shield. For more than thirty years she'd been a pillar of the community, serving as the head of the women's ministry at True Vine Missionary Baptist Church. Her faith wasn't just something she spoke about on Sundays; it was woven into the fabric of her daily life. Whether she admitted it or not, her family drew strength from her.

Episode 2

True Vine Missionary Baptist Church was a modest building with peeling paint and a towering steeple that seemed to reach the entrance to Heaven. Inside, the pews were worn but sturdy, and the stained-glass windows told stories of deliverance of the downtrodden and the power of God.

Grandma Maybell's presence was magnetic. As she entered the sanctuary, heads turned, hats nodded, and smiles spread across faces. She greeted each person warmly, her words filled with genuine care. She knew everyone by name . . . Sister Benita, Sister Alice, Deacon Willis, and so on. "Sister Maybell, how's the family?" asked Deacon

Willis as he tipped his hat. With an infectious smile, she responded, "Blessed and highly favored, Deacon! How about yours?"

The choir began their worship and praise, all voices rising in perfect harmony. Maybell took her seat at the front, her grandchildren beside her. Isaiah fidgeted, tugging at his tie, while Ivy stared at the choir with indifference. Jasmine, seated at the edge of the pew, leaned forward, as if hoping to absorb some of her mother's unwavering faith.

When it was time for the women's ministry to present their work in the community, Maybell stood with confidence and a commanding presence. She spoke about the food drive they'd organized, the scholarships they'd awarded, and the new mentorship program she'd started for young women in the community. Her voice carried a quiet authority, and even Ivy looked up from her inner thoughts, her expression softening as she watched her grandmother command the room.

Episode 3

After the service, the family gathered back at Maybell's house for Sunday dinner. The table was spread with a feast of fried chicken, collard greens, cornbread, sweet potato pie, and sweet tea. The laughter and chatter of family filled the room, but as the meal wound down, Grandma Maybell turned serious. "I want to tell you a story," she said, folding her hands, "about faith and family." The room quieted, and even Isaiah stopped playing with his fork.

Maybell began, her voice steady and rich with memory. "When I was a little girl, my mama used to wake us up before dawn to pray. She'd say, "The Lord's mercies are new every morning. You've got to start the day with Him." Back then we didn't have much. No fancy house, no fine clothes, but we had faith, and we had each other." She paused, her eyes distant, as if seeing the past unfold. "When your granddaddy and I moved to this town, we didn't know anyone, but the church took us in. They became our family, and I promised myself that I'd do the same for others, to be a light in their lives like they were for us." Her words hung in the air, resonating deeply. Jasmine blinked back her tears, and even Ivy seemed moved, her gaze fixed on her grandmother.

Episode 4

The following week, Ivy surprised everyone by volunteering to help with the church's youth program. Isaiah, inspired by his sister, offered to assist with the food drive. Jasmine, too, found herself drawn back into the fold, attending Bible study and reconnecting with the faith that she had lost.

Grandma Maybell watched it all quietly, a proud smile on her lips. She knew that faith wasn't something that you could force; it had to be nurtured like seeds planted in fertile soil. As she saw her family grow closer to one another and to God, she felt a deep sense of fulfillment.

Months passed, and the Johnson family continued to become more active in the church and their community. Ivy discovered a passion for music and joined the choir. Isaiah, ever the energetic one, started a youth basketball league. Jasmine found solace and strength in the women's ministry, leaning on the same support system her mother had built.

One Sunday evening, as the family gathered for their weekly dinner, Grandma Maybell looked around the table, her heart swelling with gratitude. She saw not just her children and grandchildren but a legacy of faith, love, and resilience that would carry on long after she was gone. "Remember this," she said, her voice soft but firm. "Faith isn't just about going to church; it's about how you live, how you love, and how you lift others. Never forget that."

The family nodded, their faces reflecting the profound truth of her words. As they joined hands to pray, the room seemed to glow with a light that came not from the chandelier above, but from the love and faith that bound them together.

Episode 5

Years later, when Grandma Maybell's time on earth came to an end, the Johnson family gathered to celebrate her life. . .and what a grand occasion it was! The church overflowed with people whose lives she had touched, each one carrying a piece of her legacy in their hearts. As Ivy stood to speak at the service, her voice steady and strong, she said, "Grandma Maybell taught us that faith is not just a Sunday thing, it's the thread that holds us together, the light that guides us, and the love that keeps us going. She'll always be with us, in every prayer, every song, and every act of kindness." In that moment it was clear: Grandma Maybell's voice of influence would echo for generations to come.

A Grandmother's Influence on the Family

The grandmother has historically served as a powerful central figure in the African American family, acting as a source of strength, guidance, and love. She is often referred to as "Big Mama," "Nana," or "Granny," and her role in the family transcends the traditional boundaries of grandparenting. Rooted in resilience and a dynamic cultural legacy, the grandmother embodies the model for survival and perseverance that African American families have carried for generations.

Grandmothers in African American families are historically seen as the guardians of family history and culture. Through their storytelling, shared experiences, and oral histories, they pass down important lessons about resilience, faith, and identity. These stories remind younger generations of the struggles and triumphs of their ancestors, reinforcing pride and unity. African American grandmothers were as much a part of the backbone of the Civil Rights movement as they were anchors in the church. They empowered their grandchildren with a sense of belonging and responsibility.

These grandmothers play an instrumental role in shaping moral values and social structure within the family. They instill a sense of discipline, respect, and hard work in their grandchildren, often taking the lead in guiding children through life's challenges. The grandmother's role is not just about nurturing but also fostering emotional strength and cultural awareness in a way that ensures that family values continue across generations.

In many African American families, grandmothers step into parental roles when necessary. Whether due to economic hardship, incarceration, illness, or death, grandmothers often become primary caregivers for their grandchildren. This shifting is not only an act of love but also a testament to their enduring strength and commitment to their families. Grandmothers provide a stable, loving, and nurturing environment for children who might otherwise face instability and an uncertain future. Their homes become beloved sanctuaries where grandchildren can feel secure and loved. They become advocates for their grandchildren in school and the community, ensuring that their voices are heard, and their needs met.

The bond between grandchildren and grandmothers in these situations is very strong. Many grandchildren develop a profound sense of gratitude and respect for their grandmothers, often viewing them as heroes and role models. The sacrifices made by these women often leave lasting impressions on their families, shaping and molding the next generation into strong, resilient, and compassionate individuals.

Spirituality is a cornerstone of the African American experience, and grandmothers frequently serve as the spiritual leaders in their families. Many African American grandmothers are deeply rooted in religious traditions, often as active members of churches or faith groups. Their influence extends far beyond weekly church services, incorporating spirituality into daily family life through prayer, Bible study, and spiritual guidance. Grandmothers use their faith as a tool to navigate life's difficulties and to inspire their families to persevere beyond life's circumstances. For many grandchildren, the sight of a praying grandmother is both a source of comfort and a lesson in the power of faith. These spiritual practices not only create a sense of hope and resilience but also build a moral foundation for grandchildren to carry throughout their lives.

Grandmothers share their wisdom, patience, and life experiences, making them invaluable companions and confidants for family members navigating personal challenges. They are the guardians of family secrets and can be trusted with information shared with them. Grandmothers also often provide advice rooted in empathy, ensuring that emotional connections are strengthened.

While African American grandmothers play a vital role in their families, their contributions often come with difficulties. Many grandmothers take on caregiving responsibilities later in life when they themselves are facing physical and financial hardships. Balancing these responsibilities while maintaining their health and well-being can be overwhelming, *but still they rise.*

Despite these difficulties, grandmothers remain unwavering in their commitment. They find ways to navigate their circumstances by relying on community, church support, and inner resilience. Their efforts emphasize the deep-rooted strength that defines their role and inspiration for the family. The legacy of African American grandmothers is profound, and they are quite remarkable. These women are often remembered as the glue that holds families together and as the architects of their family's future. The values, traditions, and life lessons they pass on to others have a ripple effect, influencing not only their grandchildren but also future generations. Their impact extends beyond their immediate families, contributing to the broader African American community by nurturing future leaders, thinkers, and change-makers.

The African American grandmother holds a unique and transformative role within the family. Her influence shapes the moral, spiritual, and cultural foundation of her descendants, ensuring that a rich legacy lives within us forever. She is a Voice of Influence.

Personal Reflections

1. What is your earliest memory of your grandmother?
2. How has your grandmother influenced your life and the life of your family?
3. What is the most meaningful lesson you learned from your grandmother?
4. What enduring legacy will or did your grandmother leave behind?
5. If you are a grandmother, how have you influenced your family?
6. What is at least one way you can honor your grandmother?
7. How will you use your life to influence others?

Mimsy Hebron is a bestselling author featured in *Voices of Hope* and *Voices of Inspiration*. Her acclaimed debut, *So You're Single, Get Over It*, showcases her wit and wisdom. A gifted poet, educator, and ordained minister, Mimsy inspires others through her writing, faith, and leadership, weaving stories of resilience, empowerment, and grace that resonate with readers worldwide.

Mistaking Refuge for Freedom

Rhetah Kwan

Your voice is your identity. It reveals everything about who you are,
how you feel, and what you stand for.

—Erin Brockovich

When I was born, I arrived in a state of pure presence. No masks, no societal conditioning, just raw connection to myself, fully connected to my heart, Soul, and the Divine.

Yet my early life felt like navigating a minefield. Every step was calculated to avoid being attacked emotionally, physically, and mentally by one of the family. Love was an unconscious dance of conditional manipulation—a fragile bargain steeped in uncertainty. Fear was the thread that wove us together and the force that tore us apart. It bound my family in unspoken ways while it unraveled everything we had the potential to be.

My first refuge appeared when I was seven years old and hiding in my mother's flower garden. In that small corner around the back of our house, behind an old fence, I could take deep breaths. I listened for the quiet, kind voices that let me know I was loved and encouraged to hold on to this feeling.

The sane voices within clashed completely with the voices of family members, teachers, and other kids. Many times, I felt crazy listening to what was demanded of me from the outside while doing my best to stay aligned with the voices within. I became an emotional eater and used food to keep me from screaming at everyone. Terrible headaches kept me from sleeping most nights, and getting fat only alienated me more.

Singing became the key that unlocked a world I had never known—a world where I felt the weight of limitations lift and a profound sense of freedom rush in. It wasn't just about the melodies or the notes; it was the way each song carried me beyond fear, self-doubt, and the confines of who I thought I was. With every lyric, every rise and fall of my voice, I felt a part of myself that had been begging to be heard. Singing didn't just open a door; it unleashed a tidal wave of liberation, reminding me that freedom isn't just something we seek—it's something we create when we dare to express the truth of our Soul.

Singing gave me the confidence to step out of the shadows and join the school choir. Soon I was singing solos and getting lead parts in the musicals. My mother paid for classical voice lessons, as she loved opera. I poured myself into the music and finally found a place to belong. I practiced for hours each day, and with each new teacher, the dream of singing for people all over the world began to manifest.

After years of voice lessons, I was three months from going on a tour of Europe with my teacher and other students. During a lesson, my teacher suddenly pulled me aside and yelled at me, "You can sing, or you can have a life, but you can't have both!" he shouted and stormed out of the room.

I had just turned seventeen and was desperately trying to release the weight I had gained. Singing was helping with this until his words hit me like a sudden earthquake. Immediately I heard the words, "You are not good enough." My mind told me this was his way of getting rid of me. My heart hurt, and I thought I would throw up. I ran to the bathroom sobbing, and he was gone when I came out.

Looking back, I imagine he gave me a challenge just to see what I would do. I failed, caving in on myself and allowing self-doubt to abandon the one thing that made me feel alive.

I spiraled downward as my passion and dream withered within me. The pain of self-betrayal cut deep into my Soul, hiding my anguish as I abandoned myself. I let myself become a victim. Feelings of unworthiness became the silent architect of my life, building walls I didn't know existed.

I was like the walking dead. I blindly followed a path that led me to jobs promising basic stability on the outside but slowly eroded my Soul. These jobs weren't career paths driven by passion; they were basic survival, chaining me to decades filled with "just getting by."

In my early forties, exhausted from building others' dreams, I realized I'd lost my connection to myself. Terrified I'd never find my way back, I vowed to change.

Bless my dear friend Michael who introduced me to David, a gentle, spiritual man, who became my lover, friend, and teacher through the world of metaphysical and Divinely guided experiences, books, and many transformational adventures. Our connection felt timeless, as if our souls had known each other long before this life. We became each other's unwavering pillars of strength, grounding and uplifting each other in ways words could never fully capture.

Our conversations gave us moments of awakening—insights that reignited the truth within. We rediscovered the voices of our heart and Soul, filled with wisdom, love, and clarity. They reminded us of who we are and guided us back to what truly matters: the freedom of profound love that resides within and shines the light on our true path.

Over time, I integrated practices, processes, and healing technologies to heal my emotional heart, achieve deep sleep, and more.

Your Turn

Step into these practices at your own pace, doing one or more, and add others each month. Committing to each of these by connecting to your heart and Soul, promise yourself this gift, and schedule it on your calendar. Hold this time as sacred. Let your family members know this is a priority and you appreciate their support.

Smile! Your body releases dopamine, endorphins, and serotonin, three hormones that make you feel good when you smile. These signal to your body that you're happy, and in turn, your cells are healthier and you feel happier.

Breathing and Meditation. Practice deep, slow breaths in and out through you nose to calm your nervous system. As you breathe in, imagine light, love, and healing flowing into you. As you breathe out, imagine all that is "not you" being released. It can be fun to visualize color to help the incoming healing and outgoing release.

Stay Present. Take a few breaths in and out through your nose. Feel your body—whether you are sitting, standing, or lying down. Nothing else is happening. When you combine breathing with this body awareness, it brings you present. This is only one of the limitless ways to ground and become more present.

Forgive Everyone and Forgive Yourself! Forgive the world for its imperfections, forgive those who faltered, and forgive yourself. Forgiveness is the path to the lightness your Soul craves. Combine your breath and meditation with saying aloud, "I forgive," naming each person, thing, or action and ending with yourself. Notice with whom you still hold energy and continue to forgive them and yourself each time until the energy you hold has vanished. This is not a race, so take your time and let your emotions come up to be seen, felt, and released. You are a precious being and deserve to release all that is holding you back from manifesting your deepest desires.

Movement. Engage daily in the right movement to reconnect with your physical body. This could be dancing, working out at the gym, exercise classes, swimming, walking, hiking, biking, yoga, playing tennis, or pickleball—and please wear the right shoes; it makes a huge difference!

Limit Exposure to Triggers. Take a break from challenging people or stressful situations! Say NO to invitations you really do not want to attend or to people. No is just as Divine as yes!

Eat Whole Food That Supports Your Body. This can be a journey, and it is worth taking. Toxins, which can be different for all of us, will throw you offtrack. I find my body is not interested in highly spicy foods, gluten, dairy, sugar, caffeine, and alcohol. It can take me months to feel good again, focus, and get back in a routine of healthy eating when I indulge in substances that are toxic for my body.

Connect with Nature. Make an appointment with nature daily. Spending time in natural settings can restore a sense of calm and safety, reducing stress and promoting inner peace. Nature gives 100 percent all the time, and we feel it body, emotions, mind, Soul, and Spirit.

With consistent practice, you can shift into higher vibration levels to be loving to yourself and attract love to you.

After many years of consistent practice, I met a woman who shared her story about building a business focused on regenerative technology to support people to achieve vital health and build a sustainable financial foundation.

We met several times, slowly getting to know each other, and we began to imagine what it would be like to work together. After several months I started considering whether this could be the path to escape the treadmill of building other people's dreams into a space where I would improve my health and design a life I could love.

Many meditations later, I decided I was strong enough to step into the unknown, take risks, and build something of my own. I was ready for a business I could build with my heart, live with purpose, and be in service to people who wanted the same thing I did—improved health, community support, and financial stability.

My newfound freedom let who I was surface, and I was able to release more than one hundred pounds—and my headaches are gone! I've been delighted to collaborate with heartfelt people all over the world as we help one another achieve vital health and well-being.

I built a thriving business, and my team grew based on the principles of trust, integrity, supporting people where they were, and helping them get what they wanted in their heart of hearts. This gave me the satisfaction of helping people, and as I shared with each person, I became stronger, more compassionate to myself and others, and more open to healing my deeper wounds.

The voice I thought I lost came back to me. Finding my voice again felt like rediscovering a lost melody—only this time, it's not through singing but by speaking and writing. Every word I write carries the same power and emotion as a note once sung from my heart. Together, they create a journey, a harmony of expression, and a song that is uniquely mine. Writing has become my new stage, my voice rising to touch hearts and Souls.

Mentoring others to reclaim their health, embrace self-love, and rediscover self-worth ignites their confidence and financial success; it empowers them to heal their wounds and go for their dreams. Together, we've inspired new hope and co-created lives of purpose and possibility for thousands.

Now I am seventy-five and grateful to serve a global team of the most loving people. I am delighted to find myself humming tunes and occasionally singing a quiet song just for me. It is my last mountain to climb and each song another step to the top.

- Have you succumbed to a refuge of voices that are not serving you?
- What is your mountain to climb?

When you make your health a top priority, you aren't merely investing in yourself—you are investing in the limitless potential of your future.

Life is change. You have a choice: You can keep being and doing what you are being and doing now or you can open the door for the life you've only dreamed about. With each step, you develop deeper self-trust, peace, and the ability to go within for the insights and gems that await you.

What you experience will lift you and others up, opening possibilities that are not visible now.

Your journey awaits—let's begin! True freedom is now!

Everything and Anything Is Possible!

—Lee Harris

Rhetah Kwan is one of those rare people you might meet once or twice in a lifetime. She's an inspiring life catalyst, speaker, certified life coach, homeopathic consultant, bestselling author, and global entrepreneur.

She focuses on educating people to live a life without limits by profoundly elevating their holistic well-being to new heights. She has helped countless individuals from all over the world recapture a level of health and vitality and build a solid economic foundation to live the life they love.

Awaken Your Voice of Love: A Free Coaching Session

As a heartfelt gift, I invite you to a transformative 45-minute coaching session designed to awaken your inner voice and ignite your passions. Step into a sacred, confidential space that honors your journey and empowers you to pursue your dreams.

How to Schedule: Visit www.RhetahKwan.com, click 'Schedule an Appointment,' and enter "Mistaking Refuge for Freedom" in the Additional Information section.

Ready to Elevate Your Life? If you're prepared to become a soul-led individual and boldly pursue your dreams, scan the QR code below to begin your journey!

Imagine the Impact: Prioritizing your health isn't just about feeling better; it's the foundation for transformative change in every aspect of your life. Your journey towards vitality will inspire not just you, but also your loved ones and community.

Join the Intuitive Journey: Embrace your instincts for profound satisfaction and remarkable results.

What to Expect:

1. **Free Health Assessment:** Download two key steps to unlock your vitality and well-being.
2. **Complimentary Session:** Discover how your daily choices shape your health and life.

Together We Rise

Cory Lopes-Warfield

My social channels combined have nearly a million followers and subscribers with millions of impressions, so I've been called a "voice of influence" on occasion, but I resonate much more with the term *impactor*. Vanity metrics alone mean very little, especially within a system that can be "gamed," but the impact that our presence makes—our content, messages, conversations, brands—is what really matters.

People talk about "adding value" on social media, but what does that really mean? If it's "teaching people stuff you know," I argue that is inherently condescending . . . and progressively less and less welcome. For me, it's all about *conversations*. Facilitating meaningful conversations where others can be heard, lend their thought leadership and perspectives, and ultimately exchange concepts, resources, and energy in a symbiotic fashion seems to be one of the drivers of my daily growth and perceived impact on social media.

This doesn't mean we can't teach what we know and are learning as well, but it's a delivery mechanism, an intention, a way of developing true connection. Connection means so much to me that I named one of my companies Coryconnects LLC, and launched a podcast by the same name. I ask every guest what connection means to them, and the answers have been varied, profound, unexpected, and awesome. I've asked founders of billion-dollar companies, gold medal Olympians, and more, and one seeming through line is the sensation of being part of something bigger than themselves.

This is one of the locks that holding the keys of "influence" can open. When we put ourselves in a position to help direct the conversations, we help shape the narrative. When we step up and put ourselves out there authentically, with purpose, and with open minds and hearts, we can truly effect a huge impact.

This impact, this "influence," is available to everyone right now, *for free*, thanks to social media. What we need to do is optimize our offerings and profiles, understand our ideal client personas and their ideal sales journey, give our growing audiences what they want (not what we want them to want), stay ahead of algorithm change, and holistically be *all in*.

We are entering an era in which AI will sell to and buy from AIs on our behalf (autonomous agents), and our *attention* is being replaced slowly but surely by our *intention*, which AI is great at predicting, particularly with the ton of personal data it has on us. We've spent a generation freely giving our data to "big tech," marketing agencies, and data aggregators with no upside for ourselves (some would postulate that there's been a downside), and now we're entering a new "era" where "we the people" tuning into it may actually find that we're able to reap some of the fruits of our data, thanks to web3 (decentralization, blockchain), AI, and emergent new business models and ways that business is done internationally.

In addition to becoming stewards of our own data, another disruptive paradigm shift I and others use our influence to impact (and hopefully effectuate) is UBI: universal basic income. There are other manifestations of the same concept; UBC (the C can stand for compute or care), CABUBI (community asset-based UBI), etc., but the point is that every human being should be receiving dividends from the work that AI and the companies using it are progressively doing more and more of instead of humans, rending our abilities to earn "wages" or monies with which to provide for ourselves and families virtually impossible within the constructs we've all grown accustomed to over the past several hundred years.

We are witnessing history in the making. Humans and technology are merging (think "cyborgs," "singularity," and human-brain interfaces), humanoid robots (androids) powered by AI are already among us and will be deployed by the millions this year. For those of us with a large reach and audiences who care what we think and say (which can be any and all of us!), helping humanity stay on the right side of all these emergent changes is our responsibility and must be our priority.

These are the types of conversations I like to initiative and promote on my social channels, and how I hope to have a positive impact on humanity. Unpacking things like UBI, super-intelligence (ASI), human-capital redundancies, the need for blockchain, and provenance of data (what of what we are fed is "real," what's AI-generated, etc.) have become a hallmark of my personal brand—and the apparent reason life "made" me an influencer.

In addition to being an influencer, I remain a serial tech founder, advisor, and executive. Some of my projects include **Agora World** (creating immersive digital twins with world-class 3D visualization), **Loving Is** (teaching algorithms and machines what love is and why it matters as a "better-for-us" way to leverage various AI the right way), **We J** (a community-based tech platform for DJs, placing music, music delivery, and music creation on the blockchain with "just enough" access to AI), **SHIZA** (creating individual language models or ILMS), **VRFD** (a "layer 0" for social media as its own platform that can push to others, where all users are assuredly humans who are who they say they are and the world content is also verified in several ways), **Tech For Good** (my newsletter on LinkedIn with more than 200K subscribers), **Coryconnects** (media outlet and viral growth coaching and marketing), and **Celestial Ascent** (an ambitious hotel project in the Middle East that brings "space tourism to earth" as a first step toward us being interplanetary). I'm also an entrepreneur in residence at the **Founder Institute**, where I've been named "Mentor In Excellence" thrice and helped numerous innovative companies launch and scale as a result of my work there.

I've included this non-exhaustive list here in this chapter not as a way to generate interest or awareness of my projects, but because I'm often asked how I'm able to be involved in so many companies as an executive, founder, or board member simultaneously, and the answer ties into this chapter. Said succinctly, it's a result of proper time management and effective use of current tools—the most obvious and prominent of which is certainly AI.

I am not one to use AI to write for me—not a word of this chapter was written by AI, unless I've somehow already merged with it, unbeknownst to myself—but I do use AI to generate marketing assets and plans, go-to-market plans, executive summaries, pitch decks, social media assets (video), product tutorials, mock customer interviews for market research and to asset competitive landscapes, proofread copy, summarize meetings I'm in (although this one can be a double-edged sword as we're quite literally just giving all that data and those insights and private communications to the companies listening to and selling them), summarize books I want the gist of without investing the hours to read them, build pipelines, make music (my favorite use case, though mostly for fun), and more.

These tasks each take most humans who are not using AI hours or even days to complete. Multiply that across the nine-plus companies I'm an integral part of, and you'll begin to understand how I'm able to multitask and complete so much even as just one person. Even though there's still a time commitment required to fact check and assess the "work" AI delivers, I'm often able to complete a dozen mission-critical tasks, each of which used to take me anywhere from two to twelve hours. This means I can get a week's worth of work done in a single day.

So far I've shared my viewpoint on influence, being an influencer, and impactor, the power of communication and connection, a slight glimpse into my vision of what the future holds, some solutions to keep us all "grounded, safe and successful," how I personally use AI tools for productivity and business growth, and a bit about myself and things I'm currently working on. My hope for you, the reader, is that as you've read this chapter, you now realize that any of us can build a personal brand around ourselves to achieve "influencer" status, but it's what we do with that impact, that privilege and responsibility, that really matters.

Staying ahead of the curve, being a part of the solution, growth hacking how to be more productive and impactful—and yes, making a lot of money—are all "on the table." The world is changing so rapidly and significantly that trying to do things the same ways that have "always worked" for us in the past is a fool's errand. We must remain creative, fluid, informed, aligned, unified, optimistic, and proactive. As I love to say routinely on my primary channel, LinkedIn, "Together We Rise!" As the saying goes, "a rising tide lifts all boats," and the tide lifts are certainly changing.

I honor you and thank you for reading this book. I pray that my chapter has brought some new perspectives and possibly even catalyzes some new behaviors. Enjoy the rest of this book as well; there are many actionable insights and fun anecdotes that allow us to live vicariously through the eyes and experiences of others, and there is much food for thought.

Cory Lopes-Warfield is a serial tech entrepreneur and tech influencer based in Rio de Janeiro by way of Chicago. A global futurist delivering keynotes on the topics of ethical AI, intelligence, and emergent tech, Cory reaches millions monthly with his messages of "Tech For Good" and "Together We Rise."

linkedin.com/in/corywarfield/

GROWTH HACK THE FUTURE WITH
REVAMPED BUSINESS MODELS AND DEEP
UNDERSTANDING OF EMERGING TECH

Embrace Your Birthright: Three Keys to Achieve Your Dreams and Soul's Purpose

Vicky McAdams

Sometimes, the seeds of our dreams planted quietly in fleeting moments emerge years later. I planted my seed on a hot, sticky afternoon in Thailand during a fourth-grade trip to an orphanage. I was nine, standing amid the echoes of laughter and quiet sorrow, when my heart made a silent promise: One day, I would adopt an Asian daughter. Three keys fueled my promise to achieve my dreams and soul's purpose: persistence, trust, and alignment.

At the time, it felt like a whimsical promise whispered into the air of childhood. But dreams have a way of unfolding from the deeper anchors within us, waiting patiently to blossom.

Thirty-two years later, that dream took root in reality.

By then, I was a wife and a mother to two sons, living in Singapore and working at the US Embassy. Yet there I was, barreling through the Cambodian jungle, tropical heat wrapped around me like a second skin. My driver, a Khmer Rouge survivor who spoke three languages, served as my interpreter. His face, lined with the traumatized stories of a culture nearly destroyed, concentrated on the zigzagging motorcycles. Venturing far from Phnom Penh, my heart pulsed with hope, fear that I might disappear and never be heard from again, and hidden disbelief that there were any children available for adoption.

My husband and sons were visiting family on a long-planned vacation in Australia while I chased a childhood dream that refused to let go despite the years, the obstacles, and the persistent voice of doubt that had tried to bury it.

Key 1: Persistence—*You are an energy being having a human experience.*

A concrete slab with a corrugated metal roof constituted the orphanage with no walls to keep out the rain. There was no electricity, no running water—only caretakers rocking hammocks with babies wrapped in scraps.

The director's response was not what I'd hoped for. "We only work with one US agency," he said, his tone polite but firm. The door slammed shut on my dream. Something inside me refused to turn away. A whisper, quieter than reason but louder than fear, told me: *Try again tomorrow.*

And so, I returned daily, helping where I could—feeding babies, signing, and smiling with non-English speaking caregivers sharing a purpose. Slowly, we built trust. The director's resolve softened with a nod that held the weight of my years of waiting. "We'll help you," he said.

And that's when I saw her.

She was so small, hardly more than a wisp of life at two months old. Her body was frail, barely weighing four pounds, but her eyes—oh, her eyes! They locked on to mine with a startling intensity, as though she could see straight into my soul and recognize the woman who had been waiting patiently for her.

But the universe wasn't done testing me yet. That day, she developed a severe infection resulting from being bathed in the same pond water as the village cows. The illness threatened to snatch her away before I even had a chance to hold her. Simultaneously, whispers spread that the Cambodian government might shut down all foreign adoptions, making our fragile progress uncertain.

I could only trust the universe. Clinging to a fraying thread, I left behind the fourteen portfolios, hoping government officials would handle them carefully. I relied on strangers to translate medical recommendations and follow through in an inefficient health system. I waited two agonizing weeks for HIV tests to determine eligibility for adoption and two months for a government's decision about adoption. But I trusted in the process, knowing that the universe guided me toward my dream.

Here's what I learned: Dreams don't have expiration dates. They weather storms, endure years of neglect, and still find their way to fruition. They test your patience and resilience, but they don't die *unless you let them*. Your dreams are not whimsical thoughts; they are the energetic blueprint of your potential. Your unconscious mind continuously nudges you toward the ideal image of your true potential and purpose.

Key 2: Alignment—*Align your subconscious beliefs with your conscious goals.*

Understand that your subconscious mind is a powerful force that either propels you toward your dreams or holds you back. By aligning your subconscious beliefs with your conscious goals, you can harness this power and pave the way for your dreams to come true.

The day finally arrived to bring our new daughter home. Still so small, she fit in my husband's palm. The yellow chiffon doll's dress she wore was a borrowed kindness, a reminder of the many hands that had carried her to this moment. Holding her fulfilled the childhood promise, proving persistence and love could manifest the longest-held dreams into reality.

But the journey didn't end there. We continued countless steps: securing a Cambodian passport, navigating the labyrinth of international visas, and applying for our daughter's US citizenship. Each step reminded me that a dream doesn't just happen—it evolves and takes on its own life. Each step unlayered self-limiting subconscious beliefs that needed to realign with my conscious goal.

This lesson became even more apparent when, years later, I found myself stepping into a new dream I never could have anticipated: becoming a grandmother.

The Second Adoption: When Dreams Find You

Following a year of COVID-19 isolation shutdowns, I traveled to Taos, New Mexico, for a Psych-K conference to reconnect with humanity. I didn't know that the conference would include the first chapter of another adoption story.

Before the event, I scheduled a massage with a gifted shamanic healer to ease my travel stiffness. As her hands worked gently, I slipped into a trancelike state, and a vivid vision that felt more real than reality overpowered me. I felt a tiny heartbeat—my future grandchild's heartbeat—pulsing against mine. The warmth of that moment filled me as though the universe had whispered, *They're coming.*

That evening, still reeling from the vision, I wandered into an artist's shop in a quiet corner of Taos. My breath stopped when I saw a painting of my vision. The heartbeat, energy, and colors were all there, rendered perfectly by an artist I had never met. I bought it without hesitation. It felt like a sign, a promise of what was to come. There and then, I set my conscious intention: "I am sharing my heart breath with my grandchild."

Nine months later, my son and his husband welcomed their newly adopted daughter into our world thirty hours after her birth. Her conception's timing aligned perfectly with my vision. Once again, I witnessed the blessing of manifested dreams—not forced but divinely timed.

Holding my granddaughter for the first time brought me back to that nine-year-old girl in Bangkok. It reminded me that when we align our subconscious beliefs with our conscious goals, we can create our dreams quickly. They arrive like miraculous gifts, like sharing my heart breath with my precious granddaughter.

Key 3: Trust—*The universe supports you as you create your life's purpose.*

What made these dreams possible wasn't just determination or resources, though both were important. It was the unwavering belief that dreams emerge from our souls for a reason. My promise at age nine wasn't coincidental; it was a glimpse of my life's purpose. And my vision in Taos wasn't just imagination—it was a calling from the universe to stay open to the miraculous.

A Path Forged Through Adversity

I wasn't born into an easy life of dreams and creative manifestation. Raised by two alcoholic parents, my loving but dysfunctional family left me feeling small and invisible without a right to my soulful purpose. By age twelve, I became the peacemaker and caretaker for my family of seven—making meals, cleaning the house, helping younger siblings with homework, and stepping into an adult role as my mother's health deteriorated.

At seventeen, I left home for college on a scholarship, determined to escape the cycle of dysfunction. I swore I would never again endure any form of abuse—physical, emotional, or sexual—and vowed to become financially independent. Those promises drove me to success, even as I carried the burden of feeling like I still didn't belong.

I became a psychiatric nurse practitioner, and for forty-five years I developed life-changing programs worldwide. I was named Nurse of the Year in Guam for creating island-wide well-baby programs and grant-based programs for victims of sexual trauma. I worked with federal judges in Hawaii, building the first intensive adolescent treatment programs as part of a class action lawsuit for special needs children. Just last year, I received a phone call from a psychiatrist working at that adolescent program I had started almost thirty-five years earlier in Hawaii—still successfully running, still changing lives.

I developed international programs in Singapore, Texas, and Hawaii, including telepsychiatry services and one of the first opioid treatment programs in Colorado. These accomplishments were not about accolades but purpose—creating systems of influence to help others heal and thrive.

Yet, despite my professional success, financial independence, and hard work, I felt small inside. I felt like I didn't belong and struggled to authenticate my purpose.

From Healing Others to Healing Myself

My transformation began after my fourth serious car accident. None of them was my fault, but they all felt like quantum wake-up calls. Standing in the parking lot after the last accident, I asked the universe: *What am I missing? What path am I meant to follow?* I knew something had to change.

I resigned from my nurse practitioner role and embarked on a new path: spiritual transformation. I transitioned from focusing on "what's wrong with people" to helping them discover what's right with them. This shift began a more profound healing process, clearing any remaining self-limiting beliefs that had kept me feeling small for so many years.

I became a Master Psych-K® facilitator and a Remote Energy® Healer. I studied spiritual practices and energy healing, reconnecting with my Celtic healing ancestral roots, and continued my twenty-year practice as a Reiki Master. These experiences deepened my understanding of how to support people as energetic beings having a human experience and learn how to live their soulful purpose and speak their truth. As a certified Dream Builder® and Energy Codes® coach, I help others align their conscious goals with their subconscious beliefs. They learn to activate their self-healing abilities and build their dreams.

Keys to Achieve Dreams and Find Purpose

My journey—from a struggling child to an adoptive mother and grandmother, transformational coach, and healer —has taught me the three keys to achieving dreams and finding purpose I've shared in this chapter: persistence, alignment, and trust.

Dreams are never random. They are glimpses of our highest potential, planted in our hearts for a reason. Your dreams are no different. Those visions that won't let go of your heart—the ones that whisper to you late at night, year after year—are not accidents. They're seeds planted in your soul, waiting for you to nurture them into reality.

If you feel the tug of a dream that won't let go, know this: It doesn't matter how long it takes. Dreams don't have expiration dates; they have gestation periods. Your job isn't to force them into being; it's to nurture them, trust the process, and step boldly into the life you came here to create.

When we live in alignment with our purpose, the universe conspires in our favor. It places people, opportunities, and even miracles in our path, gently guiding us forward. And when the time is right, those dreams become a part of our story and a testament to what's possible when we dare to believe.

I hope I've inspired you to take that first step and trust that your dreams are not just possible—they are your birthright; you deserve them. Most importantly, your dreams await *you* to bring them fully to life.

Internationally recognized transformational leader **Vicky McAdams** combines forty-five years of psychiatric expertise with energy healing mastery. Trained by luminaries Dr. Sue Morter, Mary Morrisey, and Dr. Bruce Lipton, this author and Divine Inspired Living® founder helps others break through limitations and achieve extraordinary results through revolutionary coaching and healing methods.

divineinspiredliving.com

My Pain Became My Purpose

Kathi McCarty

Home is not a place, it's a feeling.

—Cecelia Ahern

There was a time when I believed home was sacred. A safe haven. A place where love and laughter lingered in the air, where memories nestled into the walls. For me, home was a cozy 1956 cabin tucked away in the towering pines of Evergreen, Colorado. Many mornings, I woke to the soft sounds of Little Cub Creek below and the golden-pink alpenglow sunrise on Mount Blue Sky. Evenings ended in our hot tub under a sky dusted with stars, sharing heart-to-heart conversations with my two teen sons. My daughter, the oldest, was already off to college when I purchased "the cabin" as a single mom the summer of 2013.

This was more than a house. It was the center of our world. A place of belonging, independence, connection, a place to love and be loved. I had worked hard to build a life full of gratitude, and I thought this home would be my forever sanctuary.

But life was about to take an unexpected turn. A single decision that seemed sensible at the time would unravel everything I had built, forcing me onto a path I never could have imagined.

In 2016 and 2017, I had just undergone four eye surgeries in nine months due to Thyroid Eye Disease (TED), a secondary condition triggered by an autoimmune condition, Graves' disease I hadn't even known I had. In 2016, within a few months of diagnosis, I was on the verge of losing my sight entirely before my neuro-ophthalmologist monitored and saved my sight just in time. The medical interventions saved my vision, but the high costs from those procedures weighed heavily on me. As a single mother with my youngest off to college, I made what I thought was a sensible choice—to rent out my beloved mountain home to help offset those expenses.

It's ironic, really. My own body had been fighting an invisible battle, just as my home was about to become the victim of another hidden enemy.

At the time, I had no reason to suspect anything was wrong. I entrusted my home to a property management company, verbally verifying they would vet prospects for determining a final temporary tenant to live in there for one year. Everything was progressing as usual.

Then a call came just ninety days after the new tenant moved in; there was a minor maintenance issue, and repairs were in motion. The repairs were not minor, and the property manager was not honest. The ultimate outcome I discovered was dangerous activities inside and out that shattered everything. My beloved home, our sanctuary, had been turned into a meth lab. The very walls that had once held my family's laughter were now saturated with poison. Toxic residue coated every surface, seeping deep into all the porous log beams, wood floors, carpets, and every nook and cranny. The contamination levels were a staggering 239 times over the legal limit.

And just like that, my home was no longer mine.

I had assumed my homeowner's insurance would protect me, but I quickly learned that meth toxins are a contaminant common as an exclusion buried deep in the fine print of every residential policy. Even commercial property policies have their own coverage requirements that everyone should review with their carriers. Property insurance, the tenant's rental insurance policy, and even the property management company's E&O Policy refused to cover my loss.

The people I had trusted to find a responsible tenant hadn't even vetted the tenant, all while this guy had irreparably damaged my home within 90 days of moving in. When I tried to hold the management company accountable, they countersued me, keeping me tied up to emotionally exhaust me and financially drain me even more in court for eighteen months. This was a very David and Goliath situation with a multibillion-dollar global insurance company represented by predatory attorneys and me.

How was it even possible that someone like me—who had been a professional in residential, construction, and commercial lending for twenty years along with an additional ten years in management in retail banking—had never once heard of meth contamination as a risk factor in real estate?

I was uncovering a devastating truth: We are all playing Russian roulette with our properties, and most of us don't even know it.

The financial loss of my home was devastating. It was supposed to sustain my retirement. But worse than the financial blow was the heartbreak. This was supposed to be my forever home, a legacy for my children. Instead, it was condemned, uninhabitable, and permanently contaminated.

I was devastated. Numb. In shock. How could this happen? Such deceit. Such betrayal. I questioned everything and everyone. I had spent my life building a career around homeownership, but here I was, losing mine in the most unimaginable way.

Stress, I had been told, was the worst thing for an autoimmune disease like mine. And yet I was now living at a level 10 stress, battling PTSD from the harsh impact, relentless legal fight, financial wreckage, and overwhelming realization that there was almost no real recourse. I had nowhere to turn.

In resolution, I suggested the property management company buy the home from me. They refused. Instead, their experts suggested I drywall over the contamination and live in an infected home. As if my health, my safety, my future even mattered.

I had lost everything.

But even in the wreckage, something was stirring. A realization. A fire.

If I couldn't get justice for myself, I could make sure no one else ever had to experience this.

For months, I grappled with shock and anger, repeatedly replaying the events in my mind, desperate for clarity. The questions swirled: *How could this have happened? Why weren't homeowners like me protected? Why hadn't anyone warned me?*

As a professional with three decades of experience in the lending and banking industries, I was astonished that I had never encountered this risk before. I discovered that meth contamination wasn't a rare or isolated issue; it was a widespread problem affecting homes, commercial buildings of all types, across all socioeconomic and geographical boundaries. Yet it was conspicuously absent from many state real estate contracts, insurance policies, and industry regulations.

The more I searched for answers, the angrier I became.

I believe that when something is wrong, you don't just complain— you do something about it. I couldn't change what had happened to me, but maybe, just maybe, I could make sure no one else had to go through this.

I refused to let my story end in tragedy.

So in the summer of 2019, I founded the Meth Toxins Awareness Alliance, an initiative dedicated to educating property owners of all types, professionals serving the real estate industries, and civic leaders and policymakers about the very danger that had upended my life.

At first, I had no idea where to start. I wasn't a lawyer. I wasn't a politician. I was just a woman who had lost everything and refused to let it happen to someone else.

But something incredible happens when you stand up for what's right: People listen.

I started speaking out and sharing my story. I "smiled and dialed," connecting with industry leaders from my previous positions who had no idea this was even an issue. I was introduced to legislative leaders who attempted to champion legislative change, requiring mandatory meth contamination disclosures even after the property was remediated to our state standard in real estate transactions and better industry protections for property buyers and tenants. My question was: If the property is safe, what is the secret? Other contaminants like mold, radon, asbestos, and lead all required full disclosure even after full removal. Why are methamphetamine toxins handled so differently?

And slowly, momentum began to build.

People who had gone through similar experiences started reaching out or were introduced through mutual contacts. Their stories were just like mine—devastation, no insurance coverage, no legal recourse, and nowhere to turn. Some also lost their homes, their health, and their financial security. Some had unknowingly moved their families into contaminated homes, only discovering the danger when they and their children started feeling symptoms or worse, getting sick.

This wasn't just my fight anymore. It was ours together. I had the distinct honor of bringing this topic to our state legislative leaders, and with the momentum of one state senator championing Bill SB23-148 during our 2023 legislative session along with several professionals and others impacted by meth toxins, we banded together for legislative enhancements signed by our governor in June 2023. Navigating and experiencing our state process for designing and passing new laws is truly humbling and one of my proudest experiences outside of motherhood.

And I knew without a doubt that my deepest pain had just become my greatest purpose.

For more than six years, I had been houseless, moving between the homes of family and friends, house-sitting, even living out of my truck camper at times, all so I could continue building this movement. While others might have walked away, I made a choice to invest everything I had—my time, my energy, my resources—into something bigger than myself.

Because when you know the truth, you can't ignore it.

I have fought for this not because it was easy, but because it was necessary. As I looked to God, I knew there had to be a greater purpose beyond that four-letter word: *meth. Please, God, let there be a bigger message.*

Through deep reflection on my journey after my health event and the choices that led me here, I began to understand. The true impact wasn't just about meth toxins; it was about the violations of trust by those whose moral compass was completely misaligned with my core values of integrity and honesty. Their choices rocked my journey, but they did not define my path. Ultimately, I understood my message for the world: Leading with integrity today also leaves a lasting impact for generations to come.

While many still remain unaware of the hidden risks of meth contamination, awareness is finally growing. Change is happening, but it is slow. Half the states still have no policies, no protections, no disclosure requirements. And that is why I will continue to champion for protection.

I worked tirelessly with a dear friend in adult education developing a continuing education-approved course to educate real estate professionals, property managers, property owners, and those who serve this industry on the risks of meth toxins. This mission goes beyond just addressing financial loss. It is about protecting families, ensuring integrity in real estate, and providing a compass for those who need direction and, when impacted, advocating for them.

Some may wonder why I have sacrificed so much, why I have poured my own resources into something that has cost me more than it has given back. But here's the thing: I don't see this as a sacrifice. I see this mission as my calling.

I have walked through fire and found gratitude, purpose, and healing on the other side.

I have my sight.

I have the love and support of family and close friends who have carried me through.

I have a mission that is bigger than me.

I do not see myself as a victim of circumstance. I see myself as a visionary, a conduit for change.

Because change doesn't happen in comfort. It happens when we step up, speak out, and stand in the gap for those who don't yet know they need a voice.

And through these "wonky" eyes, I see so much more clearly now.

Kathi McCarty is a passionate educator, advocate, and founder of Meth Toxins Awareness Alliance, which is dedicated to raising awareness about the hidden health and financial dangers of methamphetamine contamination. After discovering that her own home had been irreparably damaged by meth toxins, Kathi turned her personal loss into a mission to protect others from facing a similar fate.

As a leading voice in meth toxin prevention, she provides vital education through Colorado's Department of Regulatory Agency (DORA) Division of Real Estate and played a key role in championing new legislation that passed in the 2023 Colorado Legislative Session.

A longtime resident of the Colorado Front Range Foothills for more than thirty years, Kathi finds joy in the outdoors and most importantly in her newest role as proud grandma of two. She is committed to creating a safer future for families, property owners of all types, and communities by ensuring awareness, education, and prevention remain at the forefront of the real estate industry. Kathi believes leading with integrity today is key to creating a safe and secure legacy for generations to come.

Did you know meth contamination can go undetected, putting your health and finances at risk? Stay ahead of hidden dangers with **complimentary access to *Home Zone Magazine*!**

- Expert advice on home safety and real estate risks
- Insights on meth contamination prevention and testing
- Tips for homeowners, renters, and real estate professionals

Claim your complimentary access now!

The Art of Failure—How to Fail Successfully

Sandra Price

I've been involved in entrepreneurship my entire life. My parents started their first restaurant in Glen Ellyn, Illinois, in 1965, when I was four. I literally grew up in the kitchen. You may think this would not be ideal for a young child, and in many ways, you may be right.

In hindsight, I have learned entrepreneurship's good, bad, and ugly. I have learned what business ownership can do for you and what it can do to you. And perhaps the best lesson I've learned repeatedly is how to fail.

Early in my career, my failures began to define me like a concrete wall I couldn't get past. Each setback seemed to confirm my deepest fears—that I wasn't cut out to be a business owner. I was destined to fail. These failures didn't just affect my business life; they began to burrow deep into my self-worth.

At the time, I struggled to separate my business's performance from my personal identity. When a project flopped or a customer relationship ended, it felt like I had personally failed, not just my business.

My self-talk became unforgiving: "You're not good enough," "You'll never figure this out," and "Everyone else is succeeding except you." These thoughts built up over time, creating my emotional concrete wall.

One of the hardest things to overcome was the fear of judgment. I worried about what others—parents, friends, and colleagues—thought about my struggles. The fear of being seen as incompetent or incapable became a tremendous burden, leading me to shy away from asking for help or admitting when I was overwhelmed. I tried to put on a brave face, but I felt stuck and isolated inside.

Compounding this was the pressure to always appear successful. In my world, success and accomplishment were assumed, so it was easy to feel like I was the only one falling behind. I compared myself to everyone who seemed to have it all figured out, and the comparison only deepened my frustration and self-doubt.

Then, one day, a customer came in to the restaurant with a huge smile on her face and tears in her eyes. She thanked me for the food we had donated to host a dinner to raise funds for therapy for her son, who had cerebral palsy. At that moment, I realized my objective was to positively impact the people around me and become a community leader. I found my "why."

I stopped viewing failure as a reflection of my inadequacy and started seeing it as a stepping stone, and I began to realize that my concrete wall wasn't as solid as it seemed. Each failure, while painful, allowed me to learn. I became a student of how to fail.

Seeking mentorship, focusing on personal growth, and giving myself permission to fail without judgment were the tools that helped me break through. I began to understand that failure doesn't define me—it refines me. It shapes my character, sharpens my skills, and strengthens my resolve. That concrete wall I once feared had become a foundation on which to build my future.

Failure is one of the few guarantees in entrepreneurship and, for that matter, in life. It is inevitable, no matter how brilliant your idea or your resources. But failure doesn't have to mean the end. In fact, it can be the foundation for something grand. The key lies in how you approach and respond to failure. We can learn to fail successfully and use the setbacks as stepping stones toward long-term goals.

Why We Fear Failure

Understanding why we fear failure personally can illuminate the steps needed to overcome it. Fear of failure often stems from deep influences; here are five of the most common:

1. **Fear of Judgment:** Many of us are conditioned to seek approval from parents, teachers, and peers from an early age. This can create a fear of being judged negatively for our mistakes. Entrepreneurs often face this fear acutely, as their failures are usually public and subject to judgment from investors, customers, and competitors.
2. **Perfectionism:** Perfectionism is an irrational expectation that intensifies the fear of failure by setting impossibly high standards. Even minor setbacks can feel catastrophic when you believe that anything less than perfection is not acceptable. This mindset stifles innovation and risk-taking, as the fear of not meeting expectations outweighs the potential rewards of trying something new.
3. **Association with Identity:** For many entrepreneurs, their business is an extension of their identity. When the business struggles, it's easy to internalize it as a personal failure. This association makes setbacks feel profoundly personal and hard to overcome.
4. **Cultural Stigma:** In some cultures, failure is heavily stigmatized and viewed as a sign of incompetence or weakness. This pressure can make entrepreneurs hesitant to take risks, and they may fear the repercussions of failure on their reputation and credibility.
5. **Fear of Uncertainty:** Failure often brings uncertainty about the future, which can be paralyzing. Entrepreneurs thrive on the ability to control certain elements and move toward their vision, so the unpredictability accompanying failure can create significant anxiety.

Overcoming the Fear of Failure

To address these fears, entrepreneurs—or anyone—must engage in practices that promote self-awareness and build resilience. It is crucial to recognize that failure is not a reflection of your worth but a necessary part of growth. Building a support network of mentors and peers who understand your journey can help alleviate the burden of judgment and provide valuable perspective.

By dismantling the root causes of fear, you can enable a mindset that sees failure not as an endpoint but as an integral part of your evolution. In doing so, you can unlock the courage to take risks, innovate, and ultimately succeed. Here are nine ways to overcome the fear of failure:

1. Reframe Your Mindset Around Failure

Thomas Edison's famous quote fueled my fire: "I have not failed. I've just found ten thousand ways that won't work."

Think of failure not as an endpoint but as a data point. Each misstep teaches you something valuable about your business and yourself. When you treat failure as part of the process rather than a loss, taking risks to innovate becomes an essential trait of entrepreneurship. Adopting this mindset to fail successfully must become a regular part of the process.

2. Plan for Failure

Planning to fail may sound absurd, but it can significantly reduce the impact on you and the situation. Just as pilots prepare for emergencies before taking off, entrepreneurs should have contingency plans for potential challenges.

Ask yourself:

- What is the worst-case scenario, and how would I handle it?
- What are the potential risks in my process or situation, and how can I mitigate them?
- Do I have a financial safety net or alternative revenue streams to cushion the blow of a setback?

Having these plans in place doesn't mean you expect to fail. It means you're prepared to adapt and pivot if things don't go as planned. This proactive approach to failure reduces panic and allows you to respond strategically rather than emotionally.

3. Fail Fast, Fail Small

One of the smartest ways to fail successfully is to fail fast so you can fail small. This is where the data points mentioned become essential. Instead of pouring all your time, energy, and resources into a single idea, product, or outcome, focus on testing your concepts incrementally.

This process is where methodologies like the Lean Startup approach are valuable. Creating a minimum viable data point allows you to test your ideas quickly and gather feedback. If the idea doesn't work, you've lost minimal resources and gained valuable insights to guide you to your next step.

Remember, small failures are easier to recover from than large ones. Think of them as controlled burns that prevent more enormous wildfires.

4. Own Your Mistakes

The successful are willing to take responsibility for their failures. When things go wrong, it's easy to blame external factors—the economy, competitors, or even your family or your team—but growth comes from looking inward and owning your role in the situation.

When you acknowledge your mistakes, you're better positioned to identify the root cause and make meaningful change. Owning mistakes also builds trust with your team, investors, and customers. People respect accountable and transparent leaders, even in the face of adversity.

5. Extract the Lessons

Every failure contains valuable lessons—if you're willing to look for them. After experiencing a setback, take time to analyze what went wrong and why. This could involve conducting a review with your team, seeking customer feedback, or even consulting a mentor or advisor.

Ask yourself:

- What assumptions did I make that were incorrect?
- What signals or red flags did I miss?
- What would I do differently next time?

Document your insights and use them to form your future decisions. The lessons you extract from failure can become your most valuable, shaping your strategies and helping you avoid repeating the same mistakes.

6. Build Resilience

Failing successfully requires you to become resilient—the ability to bounce back from adversity stronger than before. Resilience isn't something you're born with; it's a skill you can cultivate over time.

Here are a few strategies to build resilience:

- **Focus on your "why":** Reconnecting with your purpose can provide motivation to persevere through tough times.
- **Practice self-care:** Prioritize your mental and physical well-being to maintain the energy needed to navigate challenges.
- **Seek support:** Surround yourself with mentors, peers, and loved ones who can offer perspective and encouragement.
- **Develop a forward mindset:** Embrace the belief that your abilities and intelligence can be developed through effort and learning.

Resilience transforms failure from a devastating blow into a temporary setback. It allows you to keep moving forward, even when the road may be rocky.

> *I've lost almost three hundred games. Twenty-six times, I've been trusted to take the game-winning shot and missed. I've failed over and over and over again in my life. And that is why I succeed.*
> —MICHAEL JORDAN

7. Pivot Strategically

Sometimes, failure signals the need for a pivot—a fundamental change in your business strategy or model. Pivoting doesn't mean giving up; it means adapting to better align with your market or resources.

For example, many successful companies started with entirely different business models. Twitter began as a podcasting platform before pivoting to microblogging. Slack was originally a gaming company that discovered its team communication tool had broader appeal.

If your initial idea isn't working, be willing to explore alternative paths. Use the lessons from your failure to guide your pivot, ensuring that your next move is more informed and strategic.

8. Celebrate Progress, Not Just Outcomes

Failing successfully involves shifting your focus from purely results-oriented to progress-oriented thinking. Instead of measuring success solely by whether you've achieved a specific goal, recognize and celebrate the progress you've made along the way.

Did you learn a new skill, make valuable connections, or gain deeper insights into your market? These wins may not immediately translate into revenue or growth but are critical to long-term success.

9. Embrace the Long Game

Entrepreneurship is a marathon, not a sprint. One failure—or even a series of failures—doesn't define your entire career. Some of the world's most successful entrepreneurs faced repeated setbacks before achieving their breakthroughs.

- **Jeff Bezos:** Amazon wasn't profitable for years, and many of its early experiments (like the Fire Phone) were failures.
- **Sara Blakely:** Before founding Spanx, she faced countless rejections and setbacks as she worked to develop her product.
- **Elon Musk:** Both Tesla and SpaceX were on the brink of bankruptcy before eventually turning things around.

Stories like these remind us that success often requires persistence and a willingness to learn from failure. View each setback as a chapter in your story, not the final page.

Redefining Failure as a Stepping Stone

Failure is an inevitable part of entrepreneurship and in life, but it doesn't have to be fatal. By reframing your mindset, planning for setbacks, and leveraging failures as opportunities for growth, you can turn even your biggest challenges into stepping stones to success.

Remember, the most successful people aren't the ones who avoid failure—they are the ones who embrace it, learn from it, and use it to fuel their journey. So, the next time you encounter a setback, take a deep breath, extract the lessons, and move forward confidently. Failure isn't the end; it's the beginning of your next chapter.

Sandra Price, known as "The Fixer," is a business advisor and serial entrepreneur. With a finance and business administration degree and a Lean Six Sigma Master Black Belt, she excels in strategic growth and innovation, enhancing business efficiency. Her commitment to excellence drives the success of countless ventures and inspires others to achieve their business goals.

profitbuildercoaching.com

Entrepreneurs and business owners, to show my appreciation for your time, please email me at hello@thinkp4.com to receive my free e-book *Business Breakthrough Strategies: Simple Strategies to Generate More Business without Spending More Money.*

Starting Over, Starting Strong: From Financial Dependent to Financial Force

Amanda Taylor

You never thought you'd be here—reading these words, in this place, at this moment in your life. The carefully constructed plan—the one society handed you, the one you dutifully followed—has shattered. Midlife stands before you like an unwelcome stranger, bringing with it questions you never thought you'd face. *Who am I without this marriage? What happens to my financial future now? How do I rebuild when I'm starting over at forty-five, or fifty, or sixty?*

Take a deep breath. This moment—yes, this terrifying, overwhelming moment—holds a truth you're not supposed to discover. Behind the fear, beyond the uncertainty, lies an opportunity society doesn't want you to see. Your financial awakening isn't just possible; it's waiting. That voice inside you questioning everything? It's not crisis. It's clarity.

You've spent decades playing by rules you didn't write. Managing a household but not your investments. Building someone else's dreams while quietly tucking away your own. Being "good" with money by being careful, conservative, cautious. But here's what they never told you: Your greatest financial power emerges not from playing it safe, but from starting over.

This moment of financial awakening isn't just your personal journey—it's part of a historical tide that's been building for generations. Just fifty years ago, a woman couldn't even open a bank account without her husband's signature. Until 1974, a woman couldn't get a credit card in her own name. Think about that for a moment: Your mother or grandmother lived in a time when financial independence wasn't just discouraged—it was legally impossible.

The echoes of these restrictions still reverberate through our society. While the legal barriers have fallen, the psychological barriers remain firmly in place. We're only one or two generations removed from an era when women were systematically excluded from every meaningful financial decision. Our mothers couldn't get business loans. Our grandmothers couldn't buy property. The message was clear: Money wasn't women's domain.

But here's what makes this moment in history so powerful: We're witnessing the first generation of women who have both the legal right and the practical means to build wealth on their own terms. The same system that once denied women basic financial rights now watches as female investors consistently outperform their male counterparts. Companies with women at the helm deliver higher returns. Female-led investment firms are revolutionizing Wall Street's approach to wealth management.

Take Mellody Hobson, who rose from a childhood marked by financial instability to become the president of Ariel Investments and one of the most respected voices in finance. Or Sara Blakely, who maintained 100 percent ownership of Spanx from its inception, demonstrating that women can build billion-dollar enterprises while keeping complete financial control. More than just success stories, these are proof that women's natural financial instincts, when unleashed, can create extraordinary results.

The statistics tell us you're far from alone. Nearly 40 percent of women over fifty will experience the financial aftershocks of divorce, yet most will say the same thing five years later: "I wish I had taken control sooner." Not just of their divorce proceedings or their bank accounts, but of the beliefs that kept them financially dependent in the first place.

I know this path intimately, but my story might surprise you. I wasn't pushed out of my marriage; I chose to leave. There was no windfall settlement, no substantial retirement package to cushion the transition. What I did have was years of suppressed financial wisdom and investment instincts that had been overruled by the "default" decision maker in our marriage—my husband.

Here's the truth that transformed my life and can transform yours: You don't need to wait for divorce to claim your financial power. You don't need a crisis to start having conversations about money and investing. What you need is education, confidence, and the permission to trust your financial instincts.

Science confirms what many of us have quietly suspected: Women's brains are uniquely wired for superior financial decision-making. In *The Upgrade* by Louann Brizendine, the groundbreaking research reveals why. Our brains process risk differently, engaging multiple regions simultaneously to evaluate decisions from various angles. While men's brains often light up in areas associated with quick action and immediate reward, women's neural pathways activate in regions linked to long-term planning, nuanced analysis, and comprehensive risk assessment.

The data backs this up with stunning clarity. A landmark study by Fidelity Investments found that women's investment accounts outperform men's by an average of 0.4 percent annually. At first glance, this might seem modest. But compound that difference over decades, and it translates into hundreds of thousands of dollars in additional wealth. When women manage hedge funds, they outperform their male counterparts by 2 percent. According to Fidelity, during the market volatility of 2020, female-managed funds outperformed by 6 percent.

What drives these superior returns? The same traits society often dismisses as feminine "hesitation" or "overcaution." According to The Motley Fool and Fidelity Investments:

- Women trade 69 percent less frequently than men, avoiding costly fees and timing mistakes.
- Female investors are 60 percent more likely to thoroughly research their investments.

- Women are 47 percent more likely to consider concrete financial goals rather than just "beating the market."
- Female investors show higher likelihood of maintaining steady investment strategies during market volatility.

Society has convinced us to silence these natural abilities. We've been taught to defer to male partners on investment decisions, despite evidence that our approach often yields better results. We've been conditioned to doubt our financial instincts, even though these very instincts—caution mixed with calculated risk-taking, thorough research combined with intuitive understanding of value—are exactly what successful wealth-building requires.

But here's the devastating reality I witness far too often: When women do gain control of significant wealth—particularly through divorce settlements—many find themselves adrift without the financial literacy needed to preserve and grow that money. I've watched too many women receive six- and seven-figure divorce settlements only to see that money vanish within five years. These women aren't irresponsible or incapable. They're victims of a system that kept them financially illiterate by design.

Let's talk candidly about the pitfalls I've witnessed repeatedly in my work with women navigating post-divorce finances. These aren't character flaws; they're predictable outcomes of a system that deliberately keeps women financially uninformed:

The Settlement Spending Trap

Many women view their divorce settlement as a safety net rather than seed capital for their future. Without proper financial education, a million-dollar settlement can vanish with devastating speed. I've watched women purchase luxury homes outright, draining their liquid assets instead of leveraging smart mortgages to keep their capital working for them. Others fall into the lifestyle maintenance trap, trying to preserve their married standard of living without the incoming cash flow to sustain it.

The Emotional Investment Spiral

Divorce triggers a complex web of emotions that can devastate even the most substantial settlement. Fear drives women to keep everything in cash, letting inflation erode their wealth. Guilt leads to excessive spending on children, attempting to "make up" for the divorce. Revenge shopping—using retail therapy to soothe emotional wounds—can drain resources that should be used to build their future. These emotional spending triggers aren't character weaknesses; they're natural responses to trauma that need to be recognized and managed.

The Advisory Disconnect

Too often, women inherit their ex-husband's financial advisor along with their settlement. These advisors frequently continue managing the money as they did during the marriage, failing to adapt to a woman's different goals, risk tolerance, and time horizon. Worse, many women feel intimidated about questioning their advisor's strategies or admitting when they don't understand the investment approach.

But these pitfalls aren't your destiny. Let's talk about how to move forward with confidence and clarity.

Transforming Financial Knowledge into Power: Your Action Plan

The path to financial empowerment isn't about making sweeping changes overnight. It's about taking strategic, intentional steps that build both your knowledge and your confidence. Here's how to begin:

Step 1: Assess Your Current Financial Reality. Before you can move forward, you need absolute clarity about where you stand. This isn't just about numbers; it's about understanding your relationship with money.

- Create a complete inventory of your assets, including retirement accounts, investments, and property.

- Track your spending patterns for thirty days without judgment.
- List every subscription, automatic payment, and recurring expense.
- Calculate your true monthly living costs, not your aspirational budget.

Step 2: Build Your Financial Support Team. You need advocates who understand both finance and women's unique needs.

- Interview at least three financial advisors who specifically work with women.
- Look for a female CPA who specializes in wealth building, not just tax preparation.
- Join investment clubs or communities focused on women's financial education.
- Consider working with a money coach who can help address emotional spending patterns.

Step 3: Create Your Financial Education Framework. Knowledge is your greatest asset, but you need a structured approach.

- Start with one financial topic that most interests or concerns you.
- Commit to learning three new financial terms each week.
- Subscribe to financial newsletters written specifically for women.
- Set aside dedicated time each week for financial education.
- Join a community of women committed to financial literacy.

Step 4: Take Control of Your Investment Strategy. This is where many women hesitate, but it's crucial for building long-term wealth.

- Start with a small amount to invest while you're learning.
- Focus on understanding different investment vehicles (stocks, bonds, ETFs, real estate).
- Learn to read and understand basic financial statements.
- Define your personal investment criteria based on your values and goals.

- Practice creating and rebalancing a model portfolio before making major moves.

Step 5: Develop Your Wealth-Building Mindset. Success requires rewiring how you think about money and your relationship with it.

- Challenge inherited beliefs about money and women's roles.
- Document your money wins, no matter how small.
- Create specific financial goals tied to your personal value.
- Visualize yourself as a wealthy woman and notice what feelings arise.
- Address any guilt or shame around building personal wealth.

Step 6: Implement Protection Strategies. Building wealth isn't just about making money—it's about protecting it.

- Review and update all insurance policies.
- Create or update your estate plan.
- Build an emergency fund that covers twelve months of expenses.
- Understand and implement basic tax planning strategies.
- Set up regular financial review sessions with your advisory team.

Creating a Legacy of Financial Power

The impact of your financial awakening extends far beyond your own wealth. When women step into their financial power, they create ripples that transform families, communities, and future generations.

Consider this: Daughters of financially independent women are 88 percent more likely to be confident in their own financial decisions. When mothers invest, their daughters are twice as likely to invest themselves. Every time you check your portfolio, research an investment, or make a confident financial decision, you're not just building your wealth—you're reshaping what's possible for every young woman watching you.

This generational impact isn't merely about passing down money; it's about transmitting financial wisdom. Women who understand wealth building become living proof that financial power isn't a male domain. Your nieces, daughters, and granddaughters will grow up knowing that managing investments isn't just something their fathers and brothers do; it's their birthright too.

Your financial awakening—whether sparked by divorce, dissatisfaction, death, or determination—is about more than money. It's about reclaiming power that has been systematically denied to women for generations. Every time you learn about an investment strategy, make a confident financial decision, or teach another woman what you've learned, you're part of a revolutionary shift. Beyond just securing your own future, you're helping to create a world where financial power is no longer gendered. Where wealth building isn't just a man's game. Where every woman knows, deep in her bones, that she has both the right and the ability to build lasting wealth. Your journey to financial empowerment is part of a legacy that will echo through generations. The time for hesitation is over. Your financial revolution begins now.

Amanda Taylor is disrupting traditional wealth-building paradigms as a wealth strategist and mentor who guides ambitious women in building generational wealth through alternative investments. Her own journey through divorce became the catalyst that transformed her approach to financial empowerment, revealing how society's imposed limitations on women's financial power could be turned into extraordinary strengths.

A fierce advocate for financial literacy and women's economic empowerment, Amanda is pioneering a movement that transforms "feminine" traits into financial superpowers. Through her signature program, Investing 101, she equips women with the knowledge, networks, and confidence to build their financial empires. Having navigated her own path from financial dependence to independence, she brings both expertise and deep empathy to her work of helping women claim their financial power.

Amanda is passionate about challenging women to reject outdated narratives about money and embrace their natural financial abilities. Her work isn't just about building wealth—it's about creating a new generation of financially fearless women.

expandyourempire.org

7-Day Financial Confidence Challenge https://
download.expandyourempire.org/confidence

I Found My Calling: From Corporate Admin to Owner and Advocate

Heather Winandy

I never knew what I wanted to be "when I grew up." My parents would often ask me, and I just didn't have a good answer, or at least one that was impressive in my mind. I sometimes would reply with "I will work in an office and live in a condo in the city." That was not the response my parents expected—it was so generic. My dad knew when he was a kid that he would be a Navy pilot and my mom that she would be a nurse. However, being supportive, they would say, "As long as you are doing what makes you happy, we will be happy for you" and "If you love what you do, you will never work a day in your life."

Well, I wasn't focused on "happy"; I was focused on "successful." And what was successful in my mind was a big title and a large paycheck to go with it. At one point I considered being a lawyer because I was pretty good at holding my own during an argument, but my grades in high school and the pay I was making working in fast food didn't support putting myself through law school. Instead I went to the local community college (where both of my parents graduated) and enrolled in paralegal courses.

In the summer of 1993, I remember sitting in the backyard, sunning myself. I was an adult, and my dad came outside and said to me, "If you think I am going to let you sit here in the sun eating potato chips for the rest of your life, you've got another thing coming!" So

I got up—annoyed—and started looking at the want ads in an actual newspaper, circling potential opportunities in red marker, like I'd seen on TV shows. I found a posting from a staffing company and ended up getting my first corporate job through them, making $13,500 per year (I was RICH).

I worked full-time and went to school part-time. My parents said that if I came home with good grades, they would reimburse me for the cost of school. Well, I did poorly and never recouped a dime. I passed some classes, dropped out of others with failing grades, and withdrew from quite a few . . . I just wasn't ready mentally at the time. I muddled through my twenties taking a class here and there because I knew if I completely stopped, I would never finish.

I was successful in my work roles. I did my job, was a quick learner, and took on new tasks often. The problem was that I never got promoted; I was never offered more in the space of a role than what I was hired to do. This disappointed me because I knew my brain could handle more. I continued to attempt to impress my bosses by requesting more projects. Sometimes I found myself in hot water because my work would become sloppy or I would miss a deadline, but in my mind, I was shouting, "Look at everything I do around here—I am valuable!" My employers just didn't share the vision I had for myself.

I would make lists of what I was hired to do, what I had taken on, and what processes I'd improved. During review time, I would lay out where I would see myself going in the company, and inevitably my famous line would come out: "I can stay if you would promote me or I can find another company that will pay me more." About every two to four years, I found myself at a new employer, making more money but starting back at the beginning—working to impress.

I have worked for fast food, retail, small companies, family-owned firms, and large organizations. I have been laid off, fired, promoted, written up, misunderstood, admonished, cheered for, found lifelong friends, and acquired so much swag I could open up my own thrift store. But it wasn't until three decades had passed that I realized what I was here to do.

Through all of these career journeys, I learned about various industries. I learned where my limitations are, and I learned how to overcome fear of rejection. I took classes and read many self-improvement books. Throughout my career, friends, family, and colleagues would ask me for help because they saw what I was accomplishing.

"How did you get this new job so quickly? Can you teach me?"
"How do you find the courage to network? Can you teach me?"
"I need to make a new resume so I can find a better job. Can you help me?"

My answers to these questions were always "Yes, of course." I paid for coaches to learn what works and what doesn't, how to play the game, and how to overcome self-doubt. Don't get me wrong, I still find myself in a bind at times when someone else's personality and mine clash (and I still take it personally), but I know how to coach others through the struggles of doubt and dismay because I have been in the trenches. A lot of my challenges in work stemmed from how I saw myself. Depression and anxiety took up a lot of energy, but I was brought up to "suck it up." I pulled myself up by my bootstraps and continued to fight the good fight, but it was exhausting.

When I was laid off in 2013, I decided to go back to school and get my degree. I was in my late thirties and starting over again. I didn't have a piece of paper that told my next employer I was formally educated and that I could skip the line to a higher-level role. So I decided that I wasn't going to let that hold me back anymore. I enrolled in that same community college. I met with the career counselors to see what I could do with the previous courses I had taken, along with others that I had accumulated from various online programs, in an attempt to create at least an associate's degree. No luck; my gen-eds were too old. I had to take placement exams to see if I could test out of or retake entry-level classes. I ended up starting back in high school algebra in order to re-enroll. Daunting, but it didn't stop me.

I had been told my whole life, "You are so smart; you are just lazy." Another one of my favorites, "You could do so well if you would just stop procrastinating." After hearing this throughout childhood, I believed it, but now, to my surprise, I discovered I was pretty smart. But when things don't come easy to me, I prefer not to put up a fight, so I walk away from it. If I am not sure what I need to do but know I want to do it, after some time thinking in the background (procrastination), I come back to it and produce the material needed in one sitting (hyperfocus). A famous story in my parent's bag of tricks is that when I was in kindergarten, my teacher told my parents that I had been correcting her grammar. To the insult of the teacher, my mother asked, "Well, was she right?"

Fast forward to 2015—I completed my associate degree in the arts. I continued on while working full-time to achieve my BA in business administration in 2019. Following that, I started my master's, but have not pursued it to completion. Instead, I pivoted to certifications. In 2020, while sitting at home—like everyone else on the planet—I took the exam for Project Management Professional (PMP), a prestigious initial after your name in the business world. I studied for this certification for two years, then spent six months nearly nonstop quizzing myself with study buddies online. PMP is a four-hour exam with two hundred questions that is heavily monitored to eliminate cheating. I took the exam in forty-five minutes and passed on the first attempt. I was high on life that day!

Now with written proof that I was smart, capable, and driven, I was bound to be an executive at the company I worked for, right? NOPE! I still struggled to advance. All these years I had been told it was the degree that matters. Was it the school that mattered instead? Or was it being at the right place at the right time, or being supported by the right people? I won't ever know. But what I do know is that through all of these experiences, all these challenges, heartaches, and triumphs, I found my calling.

While at home during the pandemic, the company I worked for sent web-connections for discussions on mental health. It was driven through our Abilities programming of Diversity Equity and Inclusion, in which I was very active. I learned about neurodiversity, and the autism spectrum. I recognized myself in the traits that fall into these diagnoses. I chose to explore certifications for behavior therapies and life coaching to support these challenges I have struggled with and identify what I can do to support people like me.

For years I had informally mentored friends and family as a nice thing to do to help them. In the summer of 2023, I attended a seminar supporting people with disabilities. The focus was advocating for people who are not accounted for in "everyday life," providing voices to the voiceless, a guiding hand for those in need. There I had an epiphany. My whole career changed in that moment. I suddenly knew: I am here to help people. I have taken a trip into my own hardships to identify what put me there, what I can do to think differently, what I can take away from experiences that were good, bad, or ugly and turn them into fuel. I learned how to escape dark places through yoga, meditation, introspection, and asking hard questions of friends, family, and enemies so I can be the best version of myself, for myself. And that is why I started mentoring and advocating for others. It makes me so happy.

In my career, I wasn't considered a "professional" or even a "para-professional" because I didn't need a license or continuing education to maintain my role. Those roles in certain industries have career paths to follow, with every few years getting a promotion and salary increase. I was an employee for a position that needed to be filled but nothing more than that was created for me or anyone else in these supportive positions. Organizations have not developed advancement in careers for receptionists, or admins, or even facilities employees. I can help to change that.

I spent my career attempting to fit in. I had a work personality and a home personality. I put on the right clothes, spoke the language, and attended the parties, but none of that benefited me. I can take what I learned over thirty years and share with others how to navigate roles and identify opportunities that don't exist and build case studies to support the need.

I am the executive now. I left my corporate job in the fall of 2024. After much deliberation, networking, and creating, I started mentoring professionally. I spend my days now identifying opportunities where I can share my experiences and expertise. I meet with corporations to share opportunities for growth they have not thought of yet for their staff. I guide people to identify what lights their fire and hold them accountable to being their best too.

I am a mentor, an advocate, a guide. I hold your hand; I listen, advise, and support, and I couldn't be happier.

Heather Winandy is a lifelong learner with a people-first mindset. Heather spent more than thirty years in corporate America before launching MentorMe Advisors, LLC, in 2023. Her organization is dedicated to empowering people by providing personalized coaching, career navigation, and emotional regulation. Whether guiding aspiring entrepreneurs, supporting individuals climbing the corporate ladder, or helping people tackle life's daily challenges, Heather is passionate about helping others set goals, overcome obstacles, and achieve their fullest potential.

mentormeadvisors.com

If you've enjoyed reading my chapter and are interested in exploring how my services can support your personal or professional goals, I'd love to connect with you!

As a special thank-you, I'm offering a **FREE 30-minute exploratory session** with me. Use the code **VOI25** when booking your session, and we can dive into your unique needs and how I can assist you moving forward. Simply visit my website, complete the «contact me» section, and enter the code in the comments to schedule your session at no cost. I look forward to connecting!

Joyful Sales

Lynn Whitbeck

Sales is joyful! I truly believe that when you approach sales with worthy intent, a belief in the results you deliver, and securing a win-win, sales are naturally joyful. It is through sales that you get to help, serve, and create lasting impact for your clients. When you care about your client outcomes, your heart sings every time you deliver on your promise.

If you find your sales activities distasteful, or maybe you even avoid them like a root canal, then discovering a better way to sell is vital. Why? Because sales are the lifeblood of any business. Love sales or hate sales, you can't live without sales.

A Better Way to Sell

The first step on your path to a better way to sell is to examine your intent. If you are only interested in another notch in your lipstick case—stop reading. However, if you are passionate about what you do and the transformation you provide to your clients—this is for you.

When you approach sales with worthy intent, you build lifelong relationships with your prospects and subsequent clients. Worthy intent is defined by your heart first. You want to make a difference in your clients' lives and business. You give a darn!

With this heart-centered focus, you are able to build rapport more quickly, put your prospect's situation in the forefront, and quickly determine if you can serve them. You are curious and interested in your prospect's challenges, goals, and dreams. You are connecting human to human.

Your sales conversations stop being pitch fests. Instead, they are easy and natural, leading to a clear understanding of where your prospect is at: what's working, not working, and what they would love to have working. And, most important, you are able to quickly determine if you can help them.

Let's take a page from Leslie Knope of *Parks and Recreation*. Leslie is the ultimate example of what it means to sell with worthy intent. When she pitches her Harvest Festival to save the town of Pawnee, it's not about adding another feather to her cap or a trophy to her (already impressive) waffle-loving legacy. It's about making a real difference for the community she adores—yes, even the ones who complain about raccoons stealing their goldfish.

But here's the magic: Leslie doesn't roll into conversations with a slick pitch or a barrage of charts. She leads with heart. She listens to people's concerns, engages with sincerity, and makes it clear that her goal isn't to dazzle them with festival fireworks; it's to create something meaningful that solves problems and brings joy.

When a skeptical reporter questions whether the festival is going to crash and burn, Leslie doesn't pull out a hard sell. Instead, she approaches the situation with transparency, acknowledging the risks while passionately focusing on the positive impact the festival will have. She meets them where they are—skepticism and all—and builds trust through her unwavering authenticity (and maybe a little stubbornness).

The result? She wins the town over. The festival becomes a success not because of luck or slick sales tactics but because Leslie put the needs of her "prospects" first. She genuinely cared. She gave a darn.

The takeaway? Selling with worthy intent isn't about pitching. It's about connecting human to human. When you approach sales like Leslie Knope approached Pawnee's challenges—with sincerity, heart, and maybe even a waffle—you'll find that success naturally follows.

Passion and Confidence

Your second step on the journey of joyful sales begins with your passion. Are you doing what you love? I LOVE sales! I love how I get to help my clients create a consistent, repeatable, scalable sales blueprint to grow their business. And when I make a difference, my clients in turn are able to serve more of their clients with their wonderful product or service. We're creating waves of impact and goodness.

This second step requires introspection and honesty. What's your why? Why are you providing your product or service? Why does it provide a lasting solution or transformation? How does it make you feel when you deliver results to your clients? Who are your ideal clients, and why? What's the connecting through line from your passion to their transformation?

With this foundation in place, it's much easier to lean into your authentic self. This is a must. Rather than swim in a sea of sameness, you need to stand out. It's not about being flashy or pushy. Never! It's being true to your unique style, approach, and sizzle.

My sizzle is optimism, humor, and laughter. In fact, I've had people tell me I laugh too much or am too cheerful (never my clients, though). For some people, that's tied to their prism—their authentic self. It's not me. I show up with a smile on my lips, a spring in my step, and a laugh ready to bubble forth when appropriate. This does not mean I laugh at errors, missteps, or tragedies. However, my authentic self shows up as a glass-half-full kind of gal. It's who I am, and I embrace it.

How do you show up in the world? What feels natural and light? If you are not a bubbly, outgoing soul, don't fake it. I hate the phrase "fake it till you make it." It's so false. It implies trickery and manipulation. Ick!

Your true strength comes from within. Being originally authentic. Knowing your why. Believing in the powerful transformation or solution you deliver to your clients. Clear about how you make a difference.

You can't fake this. Your prospects and future clients can sense your innate belief and confidence. They can also pick up on BS faster than a dog hearing the word *walk*.

Here is a simple technique to help you stand in your own power: Create an affirmation about why you are so good at what you do—the outcomes your clients realize when working with you. This should be a single sentence, two at most. Now, every morning as soon as you wake up, say it out loud. This frames your day, and saying it out loud reinforces your mindset shift. You can also use your affirmation before you hop on a discovery call or before a sales meeting.

If you need inspiration, consider Katherine Johnson from the movie *Hidden Figures*. Katherine's passion for mathematics and her unshakable confidence in her abilities allowed her to stand out in the highly competitive, male-dominated world of NASA during the Space Race. She didn't try to blend into the "sea of sameness"; instead, she leaned into her unique style and expertise. Her "why" was crystal clear—her love for numbers, her belief in the power of space exploration, and her commitment to making a difference.

Even when faced with systemic challenges, Katherine stayed true to her authentic self. Her confidence and passion inspired trust in her work, so much so that astronaut John Glenn famously said, "Get the girl to check the numbers." That trust wasn't built on flashiness or manipulation—it was built on authenticity, passion, and a belief in the transformation she could deliver. Her ripple effect was undeniable, contributing not just to NASA's mission but to history.

Like Katherine, you have your own unique "why" and approach that sets you apart. Embrace it! Write your affirmation, say it out loud each day, and let your passion shine. The ripple effects of your authentic confidence and transformative solutions will speak for themselves.

The Joyful Win-Win

Now that you have clarity on your why, you are able to reverse engineer your product or service into your client's why. Surprise, surprise: Sales are not about you. They are about your prospects and future clients. They make the decision to work with you. Therefore, you must translate your product or service into your client's language.

Who is your ideal client? Minimize the demographics unless they are critical. Focus on their values, beliefs, and pain points. What do they want, need, or lack in relationship to your product or service? Why does it matter to them? What keeps them up late at night? What's a pain in their side? How does it impact their life, family, work, team, business, or community? What's in it for them if they can overcome, eliminate, or solve the pain? What is the goal, aspiration, or dream they ardently desire?

Your ideal client's why is your key to winning sales. It enables you to create messaging, lead magnets, outreach, discovery questions, and follow-up to close more sales with your ideal clients. It's the yellow brick road to fulfilling on your promise to make a difference and creating lasting impact for your clients.

From the beginning spark, you are on their side. You want to help and serve. You are seeking to better understand their situation and evaluate if you are a good fit. What is your prospect trying to do? Why does it matter? What would it mean to your prospect if they could achieve their desire? Will you be able help them? Do you want to work with them?

In essence, you need to go from your head to your heart. Ask the right questions to understand where your prospect is at and where they want to go. Through their answers, determine if you can make a difference. Then check your heart. Are they a good fit? It's a two-way street. A trusted partnership.

Here's the thing: Sometimes when you check your heart, the answer is no; they are not a good fit. If you force the sale, you will end up spending way too much time, energy, and stress trying to fit a square peg into a round hole.

Making Sales Is Joyful When It's a Win-Win

If you need a reminder, think of Elizabeth Bennet in *Pride and Prejudice*. Elizabeth embodies what it means to check your heart and stay true to your values. When Mr. Collins proposes, offering her security and respectability, she immediately recognizes that they are not a good fit. Forcing that partnership would have meant misery for both of them.

Contrast that with her eventual relationship with Mr. Darcy. At first, Darcy's offer feels self-serving and out of alignment with Elizabeth's values, so she firmly rejects it. But over time, Darcy demonstrates a genuine respect for Elizabeth's independence and intellect, while Elizabeth comes to appreciate Darcy's integrity and kindness. Their mutual understanding creates the foundation for a joyful, win-win partnership.

Just like Elizabeth, you don't need to force a fit. Instead, focus on understanding your ideal client's "why" and aligning it with your own. That's where the magic happens. When both sides are truly aligned, the partnership feels natural, impactful, and fulfilling.

Lasting Impact

Putting this all together builds strong, lifelong relationships, testimonials, reviews, referrals, and raving fans. It creates joyful sales.

Worthy intent is your guiding light, energy, and character conveyed to your future clients. They immediately perceive they are not a number in your eyes. Rather, you have a genuine human-to-human connection, an opportunity for their own transformation.

Your prospects and future clients are attracted to your authenticity. It feels right. You provide them a smooth and easy journey to connect with your shared values—to like you, get to know you, and build trust. It's honest and real. It's refreshing and comforting to know you will extend the same respect for their own unique style and approach.

Creating a win-win environment fosters a gateway to accelerated progress. Whatever your product or service, when you and your prospects are on the same side of the table, the flow is fluid. It's easy to say yes. Your future clients purchase on their emotions first and rationalize it later. When you make sure that you are as good a fit for them as they are for you, you take the first step to fulfilling your promise for your client's desired outcome.

My last piece of advice is this: There is never a right time; there is only now. It's time for you to embrace joyful sales. Have better sales conversations, deliver greater impact, and grow your business!

Lynn Whitbeck is the Queen of Sales. Business owners hire Lynn to ignite winning sales, because most fail to connect, capture, and close their ideal clients. Lynn is the CEO of Petite2Queen, and host of *Claim Your Career Crown* and *Get More Clients* streaming on Amazon Fire, Roku, and Apple TV.

petite2queen.com

Get your free gift>>> *Joyful Sales: Three Steps to Quickly Grow Your Business*

Moooove-ment! The Art of Dancing to Sobriety

Elias Zimianitis

Overheard in dance clubs:

"You mean you dance without getting a little tipsy?"

"You know that I dance better when I'm a little drunk, right?"

"Drinking helps my anxiety about looking foolish on the dance floor, let alone having to ask someone to dance with."

"Anyway, house music is so boring with the same beat all the time."

Excuses, excuses, excuses—it seems to me that people tend to provide excuses when they are concerned about how someone else might see them, while sobriety is about accepting yourself for who you are, not altering your state of mind (other than through natural joys).

Try it . . . you might like it.

I'm Elias, and I've been dancing to house music since I was in high school, about four decades now. House music is soulful, spiritual, artistic, and trancelike. But it's not only about house music, even though it's the dance music I prefer. For instance, when I was young, my parents took me to parties with relatives and friends from different communities in Greece, and we danced the whole night away. It was traditional Greek circle dancing with certain steps, but it was the beat we danced to. I found that the beat kept my mind from thinking so much and kept me in the present moment. I loved it and didn't think about anything except the dancing and the beat.

When I was thirteen, my family went to Greece for a baptism. My sister was to be the godmother. At the reception afterward, all the adults were on one side of a long table and the kids were on the other side. I was sitting next to my mother, right in the middle, separating the adults and children. My cousin, a distant relative, was sitting next to me and pouring beer for us and some of the other kids. Greece didn't have a strict drinking age, so we were not bothered. We started drinking to the objections of my mother sitting next to me. As that reception continued, I could see my mom turning to us and objecting some more, but I couldn't hear her—nor did I care to hear her anymore. I was free! That began a career of drinking that lasted a little over fourteen years. I chased that feeling of freedom, never fully realizing it in reality because of the consequences of alcoholism.

What I didn't do during those times of getting drunk was dance. I didn't dance and drink because I couldn't get the effect of either simultaneously! So I either went out to bars to get drunk, or I went to clubs to dance, specifically seeking out house music. Drinking and dancing didn't mix for me. When I went out drinking, the consequences didn't seem so severe. I was a happy drunk, so people didn't question me about my drinking; most of them were drinking buddies anyway.

When the consequences caught up with me, though, I was deathly afraid to drink again. I had gotten into a car accident with a parked car, and also within a couple of weeks of that incident, I had gotten a young lady pregnant. I wanted to seclude myself from the outside world, and I did that for a couple of years. After getting into therapy and subsequently stopping drinking, I followed a very regimented life; I basically went to work, went to recovery meetings, had a little bit of fellowship with recovery people, and got some sleep. That was my life. No expression; no outside activities; not much fun at all.

When I stopped going out to dance, I lost some of my joy and spontaneity in life. When I felt good enough to go out and enjoy myself soberly, I went dancing to house music at the clubs. I wasn't tempted to drink since I never drank and danced previously anyway, and once again I experienced joy and freedom. I could dance for hours on end, losing my mind and thoughts to the presence of music and movement. What a joy! I started to feel myself again, and even to this day, I so look forward to going out dancing to some house music. I'm fortunate that in my freelance photography work, my hours are very flexible, and a lot of times I photograph events that are late at night because I'm a night owl.

Big cities like Chicago and New York City are where house music got its start. It became a vital part of culture in the city, with radio stations playing it nonstop during the weekends and most clubs playing it on their dance floors. It became something of a phenomenon for me and my generation. We couldn't get enough of it.

This joy of dancing is shared and used as part of celebrations in many cultures. The one that I most resonate with is the culture of ecstatic dance in Africa. They dance to exhaustion to free themselves from their bodies and minds. In 2025, I will be traveling to Ghana to attend a house music festival with friends and acquaintances from New York, Chicago, and other cities from around the world. I am sure we will dance as much as we can.

My goal is to promote enjoying these "House Music Experiences" without alcohol or drugs, allowing people to be expressive and experience dance through sober minds in celebration of ourselves. I feel a purpose in my life today to bring this experience especially to people in recovery. I hope to share this joy of movement and dancing to get out of our heads and into our souls. Since I have been dancing sober in this house music community, I have been overjoyed to see friends of many years also get sober and enjoy their time on the dance floor again. One friend whom I met in the house music scene has had nineteen years of sobriety, and another has been sober for nine years. I've also met quite a few people in this industry, especially deejays, who I didn't know were sober just because we never got a chance to talk about it until I started hosting sober house music dance parties. They were so appreciative of such a safe and creative environment.

Having had a sober arts gallery, Sophrosyne Space (*Sophrosyne* means the "joy of living soberly"), which provided a venue for house music and dancing in a safe and sober location and also supported deejays who are clean and sober, I've branched out to providing pop-ups wherever a community would want to host an event so people can see how much fun and exciting it is to dance to house music and give their spirits a refreshing way to enjoy life. It is this MOOOOVE-MENT that I am fostering in so many communities that bring safety and sacredness to people looking to be themselves. I look forward to those of you who are interested in bringing this to your community. What a world it would be if we didn't have to worry about alcohol and drugs in an environment where we would dance with our authentic selves and with others. Thank you for your consideration and see you all on the dance floor!

Elias Zimianitis is an Amazon bestselling author, a leader in the Moooove-ment sober dance community, an award-winning storytelling photographer, and an international speaker. For more than thirty-five years, he has created photographic narratives of people's lives. Elias now applies his talents to building this Moooove-ment in the sober dance community. Elias hopes to see you on the dance floor enjoying yourselves without any mood- or mind-altering substances.

Contact me at eliaszimianitis@gmail.com to find out more about setting up a sober dance party in your community or to receive info of sober dance parties happening soon.